100 MOST DESTRUCTIVE NATURAL DISASTERS

Conceived by Marshall Editions
The Old Brewery
6 Blundell Street
London N7 9BH

ISBN 978-0-545-80859-0

Author: Anna Claybourne
Publisher: Zeta Jones
Art director: Susi Martin
Managing editor: Laura Knowles
Designed, edited, and picture researched by:
Starry Dog Books Ltd
Production: Nikki Ingram

Printed and bound in China by Toppan Leefung
Printing Ltd.

10 9 8 7 6 5 4 3 2 1   15 16 17 18 19 20

This edition first printing, January 2015

100 MOST DESTRUCTIVE NATURAL DISASTERS

■ SCHOLASTIC

CONTENTS

INTRODUCTION

At any moment, the world that seems so safe can suddenly become a very dangerous place! Mountains can explode and shower down rocks and red-hot molten lava. The ground can shake and shudder, making buildings and bridges fall down. Lightning can strike, giant hailstones can fall, and space rocks can come crashing to Earth!

Most of us don't usually see these things happening, except on the news on television. But they do still happen, all over the world. Millions of people live in disaster zones, where an earthquake, volcanic eruption, or tsunami—or all three!—could happen any day. Some areas of the world are prone to thundering avalanches or floods, others to scary sinkholes or terrible tornadoes.

UNSTABLE EARTH

We usually think of our home planet as a safe, stable place— but it's actually not quite like that. The rocks that make up the Earth's crust are constantly scraping and juddering to and fro. The weather that rolls around our atmosphere can throw all kinds of things at us—from powerful winds and sizzling heatwaves to bucketloads of rain or sudden zaps of lightning.

DESTRUCTION RATING

Each natural disaster described in this book comes with its own rating.

The least troublesome disasters

A minor disaster

You wouldn't want to be there!

Seriously bad news...

Disastrously destructive!!!

SAFER DAYS

As you read this book, you'll notice that over time, most types of natural disasters have become a little less dangerous. Long ago, a large earthquake or flood could lead to the deaths of millions of people. Today, that's much less likely—phew! With modern technology to predict them, and instant computerized communications, it's much easier to warn people what's about to happen so that they can get out of the way. If you live somewhere a tsunami, tornado, or other disaster could happen, there will probably be lots of useful warnings and safety procedures. ALWAYS follow the official advice. This book also contains tips on what to do if a disaster strikes.

KRAKATAU

BOOM!!! If you were alive in 1883, you might have been one of the millions of people who heard that sound on August 27. This was the day that Krakatau, one of the world's most violent volcanoes, blew its top in an enormous eruption in Indonesia.

◄ The eruption sent a towering plume of ash up into the sky.

BLOWN TO PIECES

This famous eruption was one of the most powerful in history. It's believed to have made one of the loudest sounds ever heard. The island volcano had been churning out ash for months. On August 26, bigger eruptions began, and the next day the whole volcano blew apart. It collapsed into the ocean, setting off tsunamis—giant waves. Dust, lava, and rock rained down, and more than 36,000 people died.

DESTRUCTION RATING

Though it killed many and destroyed an island, there have been deadlier disasters.

◄ Anak Krakatau

BABY VOLCANO

In 1928, where Krakatau had disappeared under the waves, underwater eruptions reached the surface and formed a new island. It's now called Anak Krakatau, meaning "Child of Krakatau."

MOUNT TAMBORA

The year 1816 is known as "the year without a summer." In many places, it was so cold and gloomy that crops failed and farm animals died, causing a deadly famine. But what could make summer disappear? The answer is a ginormous volcanic eruption.

DESTRUCTION RATING

This monster volcanic event caused worldwide disruption and disaster.

▼ Mount Tambora today.

INDONESIA
Borneo
Sumatra
Java ▲ Mount Tambora

▲ The red area is where ash fell in 1815.

THE VEI SCALE

Volcanologists (volcano scientists) use a scale called the VEI, or Volcanic Explosivity Index, to measure eruptions. The VEI score depends on the amount of material an eruption throws out and how far it throws it. Each interval on the scale represents a tenfold increase, so, for example, 2 is ten times bigger than 1. Tambora's 1815 eruption scored a very rare 7 on the scale.

BIG BANG

Tambora, like Krakatau, is a volcano in Indonesia. Its most famous eruption took place on April 10, 1815. The huge explosion threw 35 cubic miles (150 cubic kilometers) of rock, ash, dust, and lava into the air, making it the biggest eruption of the modern age. The whole top of the mountain blew away, leaving a giant crater or caldera. Dust and ash blasted into Earth's atmosphere and circled around the globe, blocking out sunlight for the following year. As well as causing famines, Tambora killed about 70,000 people in the local area.

MOUNT UNZEN

Japan has a lot of volcanoes, a lot of people—and not a lot of space. This can lead to catastrophe when a deadly volcano, such as Mount Unzen, suddenly erupts.

The 1792 BLAST

On May 21, 1792, one of Mount Unzen's several volcanic peaks exploded in a huge eruption. A large part of the mountain collapsed and crashed down into the ocean in an enormous landslide, causing tsunamis. Some of the waves reached an incredible 165 feet (50 meters) high—as tall as a 20-story building—as they roared across the narrow bay and smashed into coasts nearby. In all, more than 15,000 people died from the landslide and tsunamis.

▼ A huge trail of destruction was left by the pyroclastic flow of 1991.

DESTRUCTION RATING

The 1792 disaster was one of the worst in Japan's history.

1991

Unzen was still rumbling away in the 1990s. In 1991, a sudden eruption caused a pyroclastic flow—a deadly river of hot rock, ash, and volcanic gas tumbling downhill. It killed several volcanologists and journalists who were visiting the volcano. Today, Unzen is dormant, meaning "asleep"—but it could wake up.

MOUNT ST. HELENS

When a volcano starts to swell and bulge, you know it's time to leave! This happened to Mount St. Helens, in Washington, in 1980.

DESTRUCTION RATING

This famous eruption devastated the surrounding landscape.

◄ Smoke and ash billow from the volcano during its violent eruption.

STRATOVOLCANOES

What makes a volcano go BANG? The most violent eruptions happen in stratovolcanoes, which have the thickest, stickiest lava. Because the lava cannot escape easily, it builds up under high pressure, until suddenly the volcano pops.

READY TO BLOW

As the mountain bulged, there were several minor earthquakes. Then, at about 8:00 a.m. on May 18, a bigger earthquake rocked Mount St. Helens, and its north face collapsed and crashed downhill in a massive landslide. Suddenly, the volcano exploded with lava. The death toll was low—but the eruption destroyed farmland, homes, forests, roads, and railways, and killed many wild animals.

DISASTER RECORD
The Mount St. Helens landslide was the biggest in recorded history.

MOUNT KELUD

Kelud, in Indonesia, is a very active volcano that poses a deadly threat—its brimming, bright green crater lake.

▼ Crater lakes often contain volcanic chemicals that give them a greenish-blue color.

LAHARS

Many volcanoes have a big, bowl-shaped crater near the top, left by previous eruptions. The crater can fill with water to form a crater lake. If another eruption strikes, the water is released and it rushes down the mountain, mixing with the volcanic ash, lava, or rock to create thick, fast-flowing rivers of hot mud, called lahars.

DESTRUCTION RATING

This dangerous volcano is monitored constantly.

▲ A fast-moving lahar rolls through a valley.

STILL A DANGER

After Kelud's deadliest eruption, in 1919, lahars engulfed local villages and killed more than 5,000 people. Kelud has erupted many times since. After each eruption, the lake fills up again…ready for the next time.

DOWN THE PLUGHOLE

To try to make lahars less likely, Indonesia has built water pipes under the crater lake to try to drain some of the water.

MOUNT PELÉE

Early on the morning of May 8, 1902, the people of Saint-Pierre, on the Caribbean island of Martinique, watched in terror as nearby Mount Pelée suddenly exploded. Its side burst open and a huge river of red-hot gases roared toward the seaside city.

▲ Mount Pelée is still active today.

BURNING GAS

The deadly eruption was a type of pyroclastic flow made up of burning gases, billowing steam, and volcanic ash and dust. It was so hot that anything it touched—trees, buildings, and vehicles—burst into flames. More than 30,000 people in the city died as the cloud overcame them. There were only a handful of survivors, including a 10-year-old girl, who rowed a small boat along the coast to safety.

ON THE SEA

On boats in the harbor, sailors saw the horror unfold from what seemed like a safe viewpoint. But then the gas cloud rolled out over the ocean, setting ships on fire and claiming even more lives.

DESTRUCTION RATING

A dramatically deadly disaster!

▲ All that remained of Saint-Pierre after the 1902 eruption.

DISASTER RECORD
Mount Pelée's pyroclastic flow was the deadliest in history.

TAUPO

Which volcano made the biggest, most violent eruption of the last 5,000 years? It was Taupo, in New Zealand, 1,800 years ago. About 26,000 years ago, it made an even bigger blast, with a VEI score of 8 (10 times bigger than Tambora). But if you go there, all you'll see is a large, calm lake. Where did the volcano go?

Lake Taupo

NEW ZEALAND

▼ Lake Taupo lies where the volcano erupted.

DESTRUCTION RATING

Taupo's giant eruptions completely flattened the whole area.

THE BIG ONE

Taupo is a supervolcano, meaning its eruptions are HUGE. In a supervolcano, magma (melted rock) builds up underground and pushes up to the surface, until—BANG!!!—it blows. The lava, rock, and ash explode into the air and spread out, covering a wide area. In a normal volcano, erupting lava cools, collects, and creates a mountain. In a supervolcano, the blast throws so much stuff so far out of the ground that it leaves a massive hole, or caldera, instead. Over time, this caldera fills with water to create a lake.

STILL RUMBLING...

The Taupo volcano is still active. As you can imagine, volcanologists like to keep a close eye on it!

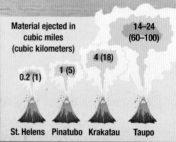

Material ejected in cubic miles (cubic kilometers)

14–24 (60–100)

4 (18)

1 (5)

0.2 (1)

St. Helens   Pinatubo   Krakatau   Taupo

LAKI

The deadliest volcanic eruption on record wasn't a big bang—it was a slow burner. Laki is one of the many vents, cracks, and domes in Iceland that connect to huge, underground magma pockets—and it's known for causing one of the world's worst-ever natural disasters.

DISASTER STRIKES

In 1783 Laki began a slow eruption that went on for eight months. In that time, it released more than 3.5 cubic miles (14 cubic kilometers) of lava. The eruption spewed toxic gases into the air, killing any farm animals or humans that breathed them in. It also caused acid rain, which destroyed crops. This caused a famine, and a quarter of Iceland's population (about 10,000 people) died. Then the gases spread farther, affecting Europe and North America, and causing more famines and a freezing winter. In the end, Laki's eruption claimed an estimated six million lives.

Laki

ICELAND

DESTRUCTION RATING

In terms of lives lost, the most destructive eruption ever.

◀ Laki looks small and insignificant, but it's the deadliest volcano ever.

NO FLIGHTS!
In 2010, a similarly long-lasting eruption in Iceland filled the skies around Europe with so much ash that planes couldn't fly and airports had to be closed.

VESUVIUS

Near Naples, in Italy, you can visit the ruins of Pompeii, an ancient Roman town destroyed by a terrifying volcanic eruption in the year 79 CE.

SURPRISE!

In 79 CE, Vesuvius had been dormant for a long time, and the Romans thought it was extinct (no longer active). So when, on August 24, ash showered onto the town of Pompeii, many people ignored it. The next day, the volcano blew up. High-speed pyroclastic flows rushed over the town, killing 16,000 people. Many were burned and buried alive as they went about their daily activities.

▼ Vesuvius is still an active and dangerous volcano, posing a risk to the city of Naples.

DESTRUCTION RATING

A very destructive and scary ancient eruption.

POMPEII PRESERVED

Eventually, Pompeii was rediscovered and excavated, and now it's a top tourist attraction. You can see many of the old streets and buildings, and even plaster casts of some of the people who were buried under the eruption.

▲ A beautifully preserved ancient street and buildings in Pompeii.

SANTORINI ERUPTION

Santorini in Greece is a ring-shaped group of islands. The middle is missing because, in about 1630 BCE, it was blown to bits in a giant volcanic eruption.

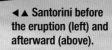

DISASTER!

Scientists have discovered that the huge eruption covered the island and surrounding seabed with a layer of lava 200 feet (60 meters) deep. A huge amount of ash must have filled the sky, blocking out the light. The volcano also caused major tsunamis that flattened nearby islands and coasts. Volcanologists give it a VEI score of 7, making it one of the biggest eruptions in human history.

◄▲ Santorini before the eruption (left) and afterward (above).

▼ The Minoans decorated their walls with beautiful wall paintings.

DESTRUCTION RATING

As well as being extremely deadly, this volcano may have destroyed a civilization.

CHANGING HISTORY

The ancient Minoans were an amazing people—advanced and artistic with a complex society and culture. They lived on Santorini and nearby Crete, and dominated Mediterranean trade. But after the eruption, their civilization declined and the culture of ancient Greece took over. If it hadn't been for the volcano, Europe's history might have been very different.

TOBA

70,000 BCE was a time of woolly mammoths and saber-toothed tigers. It was also when Toba, a supervolcano in Sumatra, Indonesia, exploded in the biggest eruption of human times. It threw out 670 cubic miles (2,800 cubic kilometers) of material, covering all of Southeast Asia in ash.

WIPED OUT

This massive eruption would have darkened the sky with ash for months or even years, killing plants and animals, and causing a freezing "volcanic winter." Some scientists have claimed this actually killed almost all of the world's humans, slashing the population from about one million to just 10,000. Others disagree. Still the volcano meant disaster for our ancestors.

▼ Lake Toba is still active and contains several volcanic islands.

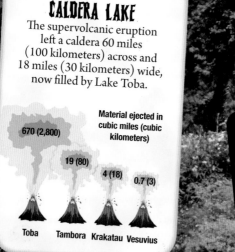

CALDERA LAKE

The supervolcanic eruption left a caldera 60 miles (100 kilometers) across and 18 miles (30 kilometers) wide, now filled by Lake Toba.

Material ejected in cubic miles (cubic kilometers)

670 (2,800)
19 (80)
4 (18)
0.7 (3)

Toba   Tambora   Krakatau   Vesuvius

DESTRUCTION RATING

Caused worldwide destruction.

YELLOWSTONE

The world's most famous supervolcano lies under Yellowstone National Park in Wyoming. It has blown up three times in the last two million years, and each time it coated much of North America with ash. If it happened again, it would be a major catastrophe—but will it?

▼ Ash fallout from Yellowstone (mya = million years ago).

1.3 mya
0.64 mya
2.2 mya

▶ The famous Grand Prismatic Spring at Yellowstone.

BULGING!

Yellowstone's eruptions have left a wide, bowl-shaped caldera, partly filled with a lake. Beneath this, volcanologists have detected a massive underground chamber filled with magma. Close monitoring of the surface has shown that it regularly bulges upward as the magma pushes from below. Some people think this means it's due to erupt again—but scientists say this is unlikely anytime soon. Phew!

COLORFUL SPRINGS

Because of the underground magma, Yellowstone has lots of hot springs and natural hot water fountains, or geysers. The water contains volcanic minerals that provide food for colorful bacteria, giving the springs and pools rainbow colors.

PINATUBO

DESTRUCTION RATING

Not as destructive as it could have been, thanks to advance warnings.

In the 1980s, Pinatubo in the Philippines was a quiet, jungle-covered volcano that had been dormant for 500 years. Many people hardly even noticed it, and the surrounding hills and forests made it hard to see. Then, in 1990, the rumblings began...

HEAVY ASH

Sadly, several hundred people did not escape the disaster. The eruption coincided with a typhoon that brought heavy rain. This mixed with the volcanic ash, making a thick, wet mixture that collected on rooftops, causing many houses to collapse.

▶ The thick ash forced people to abandon their homes.

BUILDING UP

A nearby earthquake in July 1990 was the first sign that something was happening. In March 1991, small eruptions shook the volcano itself, and it began shooting out jets of steam. In early June, a tall column of ash rose into the sky. Luckily, volcanologists were watching Pinatubo carefully, and warned that it was about to blow. Thousands of people were safely evacuated before, on June 15, a massive eruption blew the top off the volcano and sent pyroclastic flows, mudflows, and rockfalls in all directions.

▲ The 1991 eruption knocked the top off the volcano, leaving a crater.

MOUNT MERAPI

Indonesia's Mount Merapi is one of the most dangerous volcanoes of all. Active for 10,000 years, it erupts regularly and produces more pyroclastic flows than any other volcano. Yet millions of people live near it, in villages on the slopes and in nearby Yogyakarta.

2010

In October and November 2010, a long, deadly eruption of Mount Merapi churned out so much lava, ash, rock, and gas that 350,000 people had to flee their homes. This was just the latest in a long line of eruptions, many of which have been much deadlier—and there will be more to come.

OFFERINGS

Local villagers believe that leaving offerings, such as food and coins, for the spirits of the volcano will keep them safe from an eruption again.

▼ Offerings to the spirits.

DESTRUCTION RATING

This volcano is carefully monitored, so evacuations are usually possible.

DISASTER RECORD

The volcano where you're most likely to meet a pyroclastic flow. Run!

SAN FRANCISCO EARTHQUAKE

Imagine waking up at five o'clock in the morning to find your bed is shaking and your roof is falling down! That's what happened on April 18, 1906, in San Francisco, California, when a major earthquake struck.

◄ Smoke billows at the bottom of the hill.

DESTRUCTION RATING

One of the worst-ever natural disasters in the United States.

San Francisco

USA

▲ The faults between Earth's tectonic plates, with the San Andreas fault shown in red.

FIRE DISASTER

The quake itself shook the city for nearly a minute, destroying buildings and killing hundreds. It also broke gas pipes, releasing gas that ignited and caused deadly fires. One of the first victims was the fire chief, who died when a building fell on his bedroom. Without his leadership, the fires got even worse. By the time they were put out, 80 percent of the city was in ruins and 3,000 people had died.

CRACKS IN EARTH

This famous earthquake revealed a lot about how earthquakes happen. California lies on the San Andreas fault, a crack between two of the huge tectonic plates, or sections, that make up Earth's crust. Earthquakes happen when these plates grind against each other.

LOMA PRIETA EARTHQUAKE

This 1989 earthquake struck on the San Andreas fault near Santa Cruz, south of San Francisco, California. As well as flattening buildings, it cracked a bridge and a section of elevated road, making them crash down onto cars below.

HOME EARLY

When the quake hit, at about 5:00 p.m. on a Tuesday, the roads should have been busy with rush hour traffic. Luckily, there was a big baseball game that afternoon and 60,000 people were in the baseball stadium, which survived the quake.

▼ The collapsed Cypress Freeway.

DESTRUCTION RATING

Destroyed many large structures, but was less deadly than some quakes.

THE MM SCALE

Earthquake scientists, or seismologists, use the MM (Moment Magnitude) scale to measure an earthquake's energy, replacing the previously used Richter scale. Quakes scoring below 2 on the scale are barely felt, while the most violent score 9 or more. San Francisco's 1906 quake has been estimated at about 7.9, while Loma Prieta scored 6.9.

▲ The quake opened up giant cracks in the ground.

HAIYUAN EARTHQUAKE

When a massive earthquake struck right in the middle of China in 1920, the tremors were felt as far away as Norway. The epicenter, or focus, of the shaking was in Haiyuan county, where 73,000 people were killed. In all, the quake claimed more than 250,000 lives, making it one of the deadliest ever.

NORWAY

CHINA

STAY SAFE IN A QUAKE

The biggest risk in an earthquake is that something could fall on you. Here are some ways to reduce the risk:
- If you're indoors, curl up under a strong table or desk, or shelter in a doorway.
- If you're outdoors, move to an open area, away from buildings, bridges, signs, power lines, and cliffs.

▲ A map showing the quake's epicenter and range. The quake scored 7.8–8.5 on the MM scale.

FALLING DOWN

Earthquakes often make houses and bridges collapse, but the Haiyuan earthquake did much more than that—the shaking made whole hills and mountainsides crumble, causing hundreds of landslides. One landslide completely buried a village. Others tumbled into rivers, making them change course and flood the land.

DESTRUCTION RATING

One of the deadliest and most destructive earthquakes on record.

GREAT KANTO EARTHQUAKE

Earthquakes usually last only a minute or two. But when the Great Kanto earthquake struck Japan in 1923, eyewitnesses said the shaking went on for up to 10 minutes! The quake devastated Japan's capital, Tokyo, and several nearby towns.

▼ Teams begin cleaning up after the Great Kanto earthquake.

▲ Large areas of the city were completely wrecked.

DESTRUCTION RATING

Hugely devastating to life, land, and property.

MULTIPLE DISASTERS

This earthquake hit about lunchtime on Saturday, September 1. Many people were cooking over open fires. As they fled their collapsing homes in a panic, the fires spread. Hundreds of thousands of homes burned down. Meanwhile, the quake triggered a landslide that swept a village, its train station, and a passing train into the ocean, and created a 40-foot (12-meter) high tsunami that ruined thousands more houses.

REBUILDING TOKYO

After the quake, Tokyo was rebuilt. Many of the new buildings were specially designed to withstand earthquakes, and open spaces were created for people to take refuge.

SHAANXI EARTHQUAKE

When it comes to destructive earthquakes, Shaanxi takes the prize. This was the worst, deadliest, most disastrous earthquake in human history, flattening a vast area of China and killing 830,000 people.

▲ You can still see loess cave homes in China today.

DESTRUCTION RATING

Caused enormous destruction over a huge area.

THE MERCALLI SCALE

Besides the Moment Magnitude scale for measuring quakes' power, there is another scale for measuring their damaging effects—the Mercalli scale. It ranges from 1 to 12, with 1 meaning a barely noticeable quake and 12 meaning "total destruction." The Shaanxi earthquake scores an 11 on the scale.

TOTAL COLLAPSE

The earthquake, measuring about 8 on the MM scale, struck Shaanxi, eastern China, in the year 1556. Eyewitnesses described how it crumbled whole towns into rubble, made mountains collapse, and opened up gaping cracks in the ground. But the main reason it was so deadly was that millions of people in this area lived in cave dwellings carved into hillsides made of a soft, soil-like material called loess. These could not stand up to a strong quake, and collapsed.

LISBON EARTHQUAKE

On November 1, 1755, a huge earthquake shook the seabed near Lisbon in Portugal. Some 40,000 people died as buildings collapsed, including many who were in church because it was a religious holiday called All Saints' Day.

TO THE RIVER!

Lisbon is on the coast, where the Tagus River meets the ocean. To escape the falling buildings, survivors ran to the shore, only to see the water being sucked away—revealing the shipwreck-strewn seabed—a warning sign of a tsunami. Minutes later, a giant wave, up to 65 feet (20 meters) high, crashed ashore, causing even more destruction.

ANOTHER ON THE WAY?

Experts think this earthquake happened where one of Earth's tectonic plates slides under another, beneath the Atlantic Ocean. The plates here are still moving, and some seismologists predict another Lisbon earthquake could happen one day.

▼ The quake devastated one of Europe's richest and most beautiful cities.

DESTRUCTION RATING

This quake destroyed a city and badly damaged Portugal's trading power.

DISASTER RECORD

Possibly the strongest European quake on record—8.5 to 9 on the MM scale.

ANTIOCH

In ancient times, Antioch was an important and busy city. Unfortunately, it sat on a junction between four of Earth's giant tectonic plates. Their constant movement has caused many earthquakes—which might explain why Antioch is now an abandoned ruin.

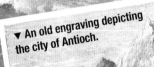

▼ An old engraving depicting the city of Antioch.

FLYING TREES

Another great Antioch earthquake, in 115 CE, was described by eyewitness Cassius Dio. He wrote: "First there came, on a sudden, a great bellowing roar, and this was followed by a tremendous quaking. The whole Earth was upheaved, and buildings leaped into the air...even trees in some cases leaped into the air, roots and all!"

THE BIG ONE

Many mighty quakes have rocked Antioch, but the worst ever was probably in 526 CE. The quake struck in the early evening on a spring day, when the city was full of visitors celebrating a religious festival. Reports at the time said every building in the city fell down, including the city's famous octagon-shaped Great Church, which was full of people. Some 250,000 were killed in the quake, and in fires that then swept through the city.

RHODES

In a big earthquake, you have to watch out for falling rocks and buildings. It must be even worse when a 100-foot (30-meter) tall statue comes toppling toward you!

DESTRUCTION RATING

Famous for destroying one of the seven wonders of the ancient world.

THE COLOSSUS FALLS

In 226 BCE, Rhodes City, on the Greek island of Rhodes, was a large, wealthy trading port. About 50 years earlier, the city had completed its pride and joy—an enormous, gleaming metal statue of the sun god, Helios, standing at the gates of the harbor. It was known as the Colossus, and was one of the seven wonders of the ancient world. But when the 226 BCE quake struck, the statue came crashing down. The death toll is unknown, but we do know many buildings collapsed.

LEGS OF THE COLOSSUS

In pictures, the Colossus is often shown standing astride the harbor entrance, with boats sailing between its legs. Actually, it stood next to the harbor—and no one knows exactly what it looked like.

MESSINA

Europe's most destructive earthquake ever hit the town of Messina, Italy, at about 5:20 a.m. on December 28, 1908. The quake's epicenter was in the sea between the Italian mainland and the island of Sicily.

DESTRUCTION RATING

Destroyed most of Messina and several other Italian towns.

▼ Survivors make their way through the ruins of the city of Messina.

SURVIVAL MIRACLE

After an earthquake, rescue teams work hard to find any survivors trapped under the fallen buildings. In Messina, lots of people were rescued this way—including two children, who were found alive an amazing 18 days after the quake.

A DARK DAY

At the time, Messina had many old houses built from rounded, uneven stones, with beams holding up heavy roofs. In the violent shaking, they fell apart in seconds and crashed to the ground. Then, huge tsunamis swept ashore on both coasts. The December sky was dark as survivors raced from their collapsed and flooded homes in their pajamas. In all, well over 100,000 people died, most of them buried under rubble.

VALDIVIA

At 3:11 p.m. on May 22, 1960, the most powerful earthquake ever recorded took place under the sea near Valdivia, Chile. Buildings crumbled, houses were flattened under landslides, and villages were swamped by tsunamis 80 feet (25 meters) tall.

Valdivia

▲The blue lines show how the tsunami waves spread all the way across the Pacific Ocean, reaching Japan.

DESTRUCTION RATING

Not as destructive as you might think, considering its power.

▼ The people of Valdivia inspect the damage to their town.

MEGA-THRUST

The quake measured about 9.5 on the Moment Magnitude scale—an absolutely enormous earthquake. It was classified as a "mega-thrust" earthquake. These are the most violent type of all. They happen when one of the plates in Earth's crust pushes underneath another, making the ground jump and heave upward.

LUCKY ESCAPE

Although the quake was huge, fatalities were lower than in some earthquakes—about 6,000 people died. Many survived thanks to foreshocks—mini-earthquakes that can happen in the lead-up to a large quake. As the ground trembled, people came out of their houses to see what was going on, so many weren't indoors when the main quake hit.

TANGSHAN

In late July 1976, in Tangshan, China, strange things began to happen. Water in wells rose and fell like a tide, or bubbled with gas, and flashing "earthquake lights," similar to lightning, were seen in the sky. These were caused by a buildup of energy in underground rocks. Then, on July 27, at 3:42 a.m., a monster earthquake struck.

DESTRUCTION RATING

Measuring 8 on the MM scale, this was one of the deadliest earthquakes ever.

ANIMAL ANTICS

Just before this earthquake, people noticed pet fish trying to jump out of their bowls! Throughout history, animals have been seen behaving oddly just before an earthquake. It's possible that they sense vibrations or detect electric fields.

▲ The modern city of Tangshan was flattened.

OUT OF ACTION

The city of Tangshan, home to more than 1.5 million people, was mostly demolished. Hospitals were destroyed, electricity was cut off, and falling buildings blocked roads, so rescuers could not reach the victims. People had to form their own rescue groups to dig each other out. Many did survive, but at least 250,000, and possibly as many as 650,000, were killed.

KOBE

One of the biggest earthquakes to strike Japan happened in the early morning of January 17, 1995. It struck the heavily populated Kobe area, where the ground shook so much that the soil mixed with underground water and became liquid.

EXPRESSWAY DISASTER

Because the quake, which measured about 7 on the MM scale, hit before dawn, many people were still in bed or preparing for work. Most of the victims were caught in collapsing homes. Many people had not yet left for work, so luckily they were not on the highway when a huge section tipped right over.

▼ This expressway was tipped onto its side.

DESTRUCTION RATING

Disastrous for Kobe, but not as bad as it could have been.

SWAYING SKYSCRAPERS

By 1995, many of the taller buildings in Japan had been designed to sway and flex during an earthquake, instead of fall down. It worked. In Kobe, many of the older, heavier buildings collapsed, while the modern skyscrapers stayed up.

SICHUAN

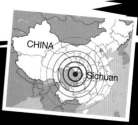

Sichuan in China is known for its mountains, wild forests, and giant pandas—not for its earthquakes. So when a huge earthquake shook it, it took people by surprise!

▲ The quake measured about 8 on the MM scale and lasted two minutes.

▲ Giant pandas had to be moved quickly from a wildlife reserve that was caught in the quake.

CHAOS!

About 15 million people lived in the affected area, which included many towns and villages, as well as the huge city of Chengdu. The quake struck at about 2:30 p.m., trapping thousands of people inside falling buildings. About 70,000 people died, along with millions of farm animals. Some 1.5 million homes fell down, and almost 5 million people were left homeless.

▼ Just one of the many buildings the deadly Sichuan earthquake destroyed.

EXPENSIVE EARTHQUAKES

The Sichuan earthquake was one of the most expensive ever. China spent almost 140 billion dollars rebuilding structures such as houses, schools, hospitals, roads, water pipes, and bridges.

DESTRUCTION RATING

Terrible loss of life, and one of the costliest earthquakes ever.

CHILE 2010

In February 2010, 40 years after the famous Valdivia earthquake, another ginormous mega-thrust quake shook Chile. Its epicenter was in the middle of the country, and it affected Argentina as well.

DESTRUCTION RATING

Caused a lot of damage, but much of it was not deadly.

QUAKE-PROOFING

The huge quake scored 8.8 on the MM scale. Along with fires and tsunamis, it caused damage over a vast area. Electricity, gas, and roads were cut off, buildings and bridges were damaged, and 1.5 million people had to leave their homes while the mess was cleared up. Yet loss of life was low, with a death toll of about 500. After 1960, Chile had introduced strict building rules to make buildings safer in earthquakes, so far fewer fell down.

▶ Many buildings were ruined, but a lot of them did not completely collapse, which meant people could escape.

VIA DE EVACUACION TSUNAMI
EVACUATION ROUTE

▲ This sign in Chile shows an escape route in case of a tsunami caused by an earthquake.

TSUNAMI WARNING

Previous earthquakes had shown the world how tsunamis can spread across oceans. This time, other countries around the Pacific Ocean issued tsunami warnings to make sure people moved away from coasts.

HAITI

Building laws helped a lot of people survive Chile's 2010 earthquake. But Haiti didn't have these laws. When a quake struck its capital, Port-au-Prince, in 2010, millions of poor people were living in shanty towns and didn't stand a chance.

SHALLOW QUAKE

Although the Haiti earthquake had an MM score of 7, it was a shallow earthquake. It struck only about 8 miles (13 kilometers) below-ground. This meant more of the earthquake's energy reached the surface, so the shaking was very severe.

▲ Survivors in Port-au-Prince walk through their devastated town four days after the earthquake.

▲ Sniffer dogs helped to detect where people were buried.

FLATTENED

Thousands of homes, many made of concrete, fell down across the city and the surrounding area. So did larger buildings, such as churches and the presidential palace. Huge numbers of people were trapped underneath, and damage to roads, the harbor, and the airport meant rescuers couldn't reach them for days. Lacking aid, many survivors died from their injuries, starvation, or disease.

DESTRUCTION RATING

This terrifying earthquake destroyed a city and killed between 100,000 and 250,000 people.

CHRISTCHURCH

In 2010 and 2011, two large earthquakes struck Christchurch, New Zealand. The first was a 7.2 MM earthquake, which damaged a lot of buildings but took no lives. The second, in February 2011, had an MM of 6.3, but it was just 2.5 miles (4 kilometers) deep.

◄ New Zealand lies along a plate boundary (shown in red), putting it at risk of earthquakes.

NEW ZEALAND

▲ The violent shaking turned the solid ground under this car to liquid, trapping it in a hole.

DESTRUCTION RATING

The quake caused a lot of damage and was one of New Zealand's worst ever natural disasters.

EARTHQUAKE SWARM

Besides the two big quakes, Christchurch suffered a series of tremors, foreshocks, and aftershocks that went on for about a year. This is known as an "earthquake swarm." It happens when Earth's plates slide and grind past each other with a series of jolts and shudders.

LIQUEFACTION

The violent shaking made many houses sink into the ground, as the silty soil mixed with underground water and became liquefied. Streets and gardens were buried under the soggy, muddy silt as houses tilted and caved in.

HURRICANE KATRINA

Hurricane Katrina was one of the biggest, most powerful storms in history. It swirled across the Atlantic Ocean in the summer of 2005, and roared ashore in the southern states of Louisiana and Mississippi. The racing winds tore buildings apart, but the worst danger came from the storm surge—a sea level rise caused by the wind.

▶ In New Orleans, Louisiana, water poured over the sea defenses (levees) and flooded the city.

◀ This satellite view shows Hurricane Katrina approaching land.

WHAT IS A HURRICANE?

Hurricanes are very large, spiraling wind and rain storms that form over warm oceans. As the storm clouds spin and swirl, they pick up speed— the fastest hurricane winds can reach more than 190 miles (300 kilometers) per hour.

GET OUT!

Hurricanes are closely tracked by satellite as they form and approach land, so people know when one is on the way. In the days before Katrina struck the coast, many states arranged evacuations and set up storm shelters—but not everyone left in time.

HURRICANE MITCH

Hurricane Mitch was one of the deadliest Atlantic hurricanes in history. It formed in the Caribbean Sea on October 22, 1998, and came ashore in Central America, where it wreaked havoc.

RAINSTORM

The destruction was mainly caused by rain—an INCREDIBLE amount of rain! As the storm passed over the countries of Honduras, Guatemala, and Nicaragua, it dropped at least 35 inches (900 millimeters) of rain—some say more. This caused disastrous floods and landslides that killed more than 11,000 people.

▼ A photo taken in Honduras after the rain and flooding brought by Hurricane Mitch.

DESTRUCTION RATING

A very deadly and scary hurricane.

HURRICANE NAMES

Like Katrina, Hurricane Mitch had its own name. Weather scientists give hurricanes, cyclones, and typhoons names so that they are easy to identify, especially when there are several around at once. Both boys' and girls' names are used, and if a storm becomes very large and well-known, its name does not get used again.

GREAT HURRICANE

In 1780, before the days of satellites or advanced weather forecasting computers, a huge hurricane swept across the islands of the Caribbean without warning. Known as the Great Hurricane, it was famously deadly, killing more than 20,000 people.

▼ An illustration showing British ships caught in the Great Hurricane.

WAR AT SEA

At the time the hurricane struck, British and French ships were in the Caribbean fighting in the American Revolutionary War. The hurricane sank dozens of ships and killed thousands of sailors.

PUERTO RICO
MARTINIQUE
SAINT LUCIA
BARBADOS

Caribbean Sea

▶ The Great Hurricane swept through the Caribbean islands.

ISLAND DESTRUCTION

Hurricanes usually lose a lot of their energy and calm down once they hit land. But the Great Hurricane passed over a lot of small islands, which didn't have this effect. On some islands, the unbearably powerful winds flattened every house, and swept objects and people into the sky.

DESTRUCTION RATING

A terrible killer storm that completely destroyed whole islands.

GALVESTON HURRICANE

Galveston is a city on an island just off the coast of Texas. In 1900 it was a major port— but at only 8 feet (2.5 meters) above sea level, it was at risk from hurricanes coming in from the Atlantic.

WE'RE NOT WORRIED!

Some people said that as the city had survived so far, everything would be fine. They were wrong! On September 8, 1900, a big hurricane approached, bringing a giant storm surge. Waves washed right over the island, sweeping away almost all of its buildings. About 8,000 of the city's 36,000 population died.

THE HURRICANE SCALE

A scale called the Saffir-Simpson hurricane scale is used to rate hurricanes from 1 to 5, depending on wind speeds. The Galveston hurricane was probably a 4.

▼ Today, Galveston has been rebuilt as a modern city.

▶ This house in Galveston was turned over by the hurricane.

DESTRUCTION RATING

A terrifying killer hurricane.

BHOLA CYCLONE

DESTRUCTION RATING

Devastated a wide area and killed more people than any other storm.

The worst case of a big hurricane hitting a low-lying island happened in East Pakistan (now Bangladesh) in 1970. Known as the Bhola Cyclone, it caused the most damage on the large island of Bhola.

▼ Today, Bangladesh has thousands of concrete cyclone shelters.

EAST PAKISTAN (now BANGLADESH)

INDIA

◄ **Path of the cyclone.**

A NEW COUNTRY

After the cyclone, many people thought Pakistan's government hadn't helped them fast enough. This led them to fight for independence, and in 1971 East Pakistan became the new country of Bangladesh.

TAKEN BY SURPRISE

The cyclone formed over the Indian Ocean. Ships sent warnings that it was on the way, but many people did not get the message. The deadly storm surge flooded over their homes and farmland, and swept away whole towns. No one knows exactly how many people died, but it's thought to be up to half a million, making this probably the deadliest storm ever.

TYPHOON NINA

WHY SO RAINY?
Cyclonic storms, such as typhoons, start over warm oceans, where a lot of water is evaporating from the ocean into the air. This forms a huge swirl of heavy rainclouds.

In the Pacific Ocean, cyclonic storms are called typhoons. Typhoon Nina, in 1975, was a supertyphoon, equivalent to a category 4 or 5 hurricane. It swept into China from the Pacific Ocean, bringing rain, rain, and more rain.

DAM DISASTER

Around the Banqiao hydroelectric dam, more than 40 inches (1 meter) of rain fell in one day. The dam could not hold back this much water, and it burst. A wave 30 feet (10 meters) high roared down the valley, submerging villages. About 150,000 people were killed by the flood, the famine that followed, and diseases spread by dirty water.

CHINA

Banqiao dam

Taiwan

DESTRUCTION RATING

A horribly unexpected and deadly disaster with no evacuation.

▲ The path taken by Typhoon Nina.

DISASTER RECORD
The worst dam-related disaster ever.

TYPHOON MORAKOT

Typhoon Morakot was the worst-ever typhoon to strike the island of Taiwan. It hit in August 2009, after forming in the Pacific Ocean, and created floods and mudslides that killed nearly 1,000 people.

HOTEL HORROR

During Typhoon Morakot, a riverside hotel famously leaned forward and fell into the river with a huge splash. The river had flooded its foundations, making them unstable. Luckily, the 300 guests and all the staff got out in time.

◀ Rescuers reach a car trapped in floods in China during Typhoon Morakot.

DESTRUCTION RATING

A serious disaster for Taiwan.

RECORD RAIN

This was one of the rainiest storms on record, dropping more than 8 feet (2.5 meters) of rain on Taiwan. The floods washed away villages or caused landslides that buried them. Many of the survivors were trapped under rubble or cut off from rescuers by floods. But once the government sent soldiers and helicopters to look for them, a large number were rescued.

TAIWAN

◀ A satellite image of Typhoon Morakot passing over Taiwan.

TYPHOON HAIYAN

Typhoon Haiyan, also called Yolanda, struck the Philippines in November 2013. This monster supertyphoon was the most powerful cyclonic storm ever to hit land. It also contained some of the fastest hurricane winds ever recorded—195 miles (315 kilometers) per hour.

TACLOBAN

The Philippines is made up of thousands of islands, and the storm caused the most destruction on two of them: Samar and Leyte. The terrifying destruction in Tacloban, a city on Leyte, was reported around the world. Most of the city was flooded by the storm surge. Houses and buildings, including the airport, were washed away, and cars were piled up in heaps. Tacloban probably suffered the worst damage because of its low-lying areas.

▼ The storm washed this huge boat onto the land in the city of Tacloban.

TOMI ELEGANCE

THE WORLD HELPS

As in many natural disasters, other countries around the world sent medical teams, food, water, supplies, and money to help the country recover. Many people donated money or traveled to the Philippines to help.

► Aid workers transport supplies to help the typhoon victims.

TRI-STATE TORNADO

A tornado is a small but powerful swirling windstorm. As it moves along, it can smash buildings to pieces and sweep objects, people, and animals into the air. Most tornadoes don't last long, but the Tri-State Tornado of 1925 did. It was the biggest, longest-lasting tornado ever recorded.

▼ The remains of one of the many homes destroyed by the Tri-State Tornado.

HOW TORNADOES WORK

Tornadoes form during thunderstorms, when warm and cool air start to spiral around each other. The wind forms a rotating funnel that stretches down to the ground. Most tornadoes appear in spring, in a part of the United States known as Tornado Alley—but they can happen anywhere in the world.

Tornado Alley

▲ Tornado Alley stretches across the middle of the United States.

PATH OF DESTRUCTION

In 1925, tornadoes were hard to forecast, so the Tri-State Tornado took people by surprise when it appeared in Missouri, then roared across Illinois and Indiana. The storm was so big and wide that at first people didn't realize it was a tornado. Towns were completely destroyed, tree trunks were snapped, whole houses blew away, and objects were picked up and later found hundreds of miles away. The tornado killed nearly 700 people.

DESTRUCTION RATING

The deadliest tornado in US history, it flattened buildings across three states.

NATCHEZ TORNADO

Another deadly historic tornado struck the city of Natchez, Mississippi, in 1840. Most of the 317 people who died were in boats on the Mississippi River when the huge tornado landed.

TORNADO SCALE

The Fujita Scale ranks tornadoes based on how powerful and destructive they are. It ranges from F0, a mild tornado, to F5, a monster with winds up to 310 miles (500 kilometers) per hour. Tri-State and Natchez were probably both F5 tornadoes.

▼ Riverboats such as these have steamed up and down the Mississippi for centuries.

▼ The wide Mississippi River is close to the city of Natchez.

DESTRUCTION RATING

Remembered as a powerful tornado that terrorized a city.

RIVER TORNADO

The tornado began by moving along the Mississippi. The river water was sucked up into a towering waterspout, and the trees on both riverbanks were torn out of the ground. Then the tornado approached Natchez and the many boats anchored there. It flipped and sank dozens of boats, and lifted others right out of the water, flinging them ashore. After that, the tornado moved inland through Natchez, causing more devastation by wrecking houses.

BANGLADESH TORNADO

The worst killer tornado in history struck Bangladesh in 1989. Also known as the Daulatpur-Saturia Tornado, it's thought it was up to 1 mile (1.6 kilometers) wide, and it tore a path 50 miles (80 kilometers) long between the towns of Daulatpur and Saturia.

TORNADO COUNTRY

Bangladesh is one of the few parts of the world, along with North America, where tornadoes happen regularly.

DESTRUCTION RATING

Killed about 1,300 people and flattened a huge area.

BANGLADESH

Daulatpur • · · ·▶ Saturia

▲ Bangladesh is shown in red.

▲ The path taken by the tornado is shown in blue.

POOR HOUSING

Poorer countries often lack warning systems and have many unstable buildings. The Bangladesh Tornado moved through a built-up, populated part of Bangladesh, but most people lived in small homes with weak walls and roofs. The tornado razed the towns in its path to the ground. Nothing was left standing except a few trees.

▲ In 2013 people were ordered to evacuate as another storm approached.

JOPLIN TORNADO

DESTRUCTION RATING

More than 160 people died and huge damage was done by this deadly tornado.

Tornado Alley has a lot of farmland, so people often think tornadoes don't hit cities—but they do. In 2011, a huge tornado landed right on the city of Joplin, Missouri, home to 50,000 people, and tore through its center.

F5 DESTRUCTION

The destruction caused by this tornado put it firmly in the F5 category. Houses were ripped apart, roofs flew off, and a large hospital was so badly damaged that it had to be torn down. The wind, which was described as sounding like "a roaring, thundering freight train," ripped the road surface right off, lifted cars and trucks into the air, and blasted twigs and other objects deep into the sides of buildings.

▼ The entrance to an underground tornado shelter.

▼ Destruction after the 2011 Joplin Tornado.

TORNADO SHELTERS

Many places in Tornado Alley now have tornado shelters. These may be concrete rooms built inside houses, or underground bunkers built in backyards. When a tornado is coming, loud sirens warn everyone so they can get into the shelters in time.

MALTA TORNADO

Tornadoes are rare in Europe, but they do happen. The island of Malta, in the Mediterranean Sea, has seen quite a few. The most famous, in the 1550s, started as a waterspout.

GRAND HARBOUR DISASTER

As the waterspout formed out at sea, a fleet of ships was sitting in the Grand Harbour, about to go into battle. The ships belonged to the famous Knights of Malta, a military order of knights. Suddenly, the waterspout came tearing into the harbor, sucking up water as it went, and overturned and sank most of the ships, killing about 600 people. It then moved inland.

◄ This huge waterspout was caught on camera in 1969.

▼ Despite the disaster, the Grand Harbour continued to be used, and Malta's capital city, Valletta, was built beside it.

DESTRUCTION RATING

Destructive waterspout that caused great loss of life.

WATERSPOUTS

A waterspout happens when a tornado sucks up water from a river, sea, or ocean. It can be very scary, looking like a towering, watery snake. Most waterspouts last only a short time, though, and they are usually less harmful than tornadoes on land.

2006 TORNADO OUTBREAK

The cluster of tornadoes that stormed through America's Tornado Alley in 2006 has gone down in history as a truly terrifying event. It also holds the record for carrying a human the farthest through the air and dropping them back down again—alive!

DESTRUCTION RATING

A destructive tornado outbreak, but most of the tornadoes were mild.

99 TORNADOES

Tornadoes sometimes occur in groups or "outbreaks." The 2006 outbreak went on for four days, from March 9 to March 13, and featured a mind-boggling 99 tornadoes. In all, the deadly cluster affected seven states, with some tornadoes reaching F4 on the Fujita scale. In Fordland, Missouri, on the night of March 12, Matt Suter was in his mobile home when a tornado roared past and blew his home apart. Suter was knocked unconscious and lifted into the air. When he woke up, he was lying in a field about 1,300 feet (400 meters) away. His only injury was a cut on his head.

FLYING PONY

Another famous tornado flight took place in 1955. A tornado in South Dakota carried nine-year-old Sharon Weron, and the pony she was riding, about 1,000 feet (300 meters) through the air before they landed safely on a hill.

▲ A tornado roaring toward you is a terrifying sight!

HUANG HE FLOOD

The flooding of China's Huang He (or Yellow River) in 1931 was one of the worst natural disasters in world history. It's thought that the floods killed as many as four million people.

SILTY!

The Huang He is named for the yellow, muddy silt that washes from the banks into the river. As the river gets wider and slows down, it drops the silt, filling up the riverbed and making the river shallower. This makes flooding much worse, because the river can't hold as much water.

DESTRUCTION RATING

The most disastrous flood of modern times.

▲ The muddy, yellow water that flows into the Huang He.

SNOW AND RAIN

The snowy winter of 1930 to 1931 was followed by a rainy spring and summer. The rain and melting snow began to overwhelm the smaller rivers that flow into the Huang He. Farmers had built levees along the big river, and a huge amount of water collected in front of them. When the river burst, it swamped the vast, flat, surrounding area, washing away villages, farms, and millions of people.

▲ People gather (below) to watch as water thunders out of a dam on the Huang He in an operation to clear out mud and sand.

YANGTZE FLOODS

Like the Huang He, China's Yangtze River flows through a floodplain where millions of people live, despite the floods. One flood, in 1935, killed about 140,000 people, and affected 10 million. Deadly floods also occurred in 1931, 1949, 1954, and 1998, despite a huge rescue effort.

▼ In 2010, the Yangtze River flooded again. Water flowed waist-high through Xianning.

▼ Water flowing through the Three Gorges Dam during a flood season.

BIG DAM

In the 1990s, China started building the Three Gorges Dam—one of the biggest dams in the world—to control the flow of the Yangtze and help prevent floods (as well as provide hydroelectric power). It's thought that the dam stopped summer floods in 2010 from being as deadly as they could have been.

WHY LIVE THERE?

Large rivers often have a wide floodplain that floods naturally every so often. But because the rivers are important trade routes, people tend to build towns and cities near them. The rivers provide water, too, which means the land is good for farming. China also has a very large population, and the people have to live somewhere, so the floodplains end up crowded.

VARGAS DISASTER

Vargas is an area of Venezuela where towns lie sandwiched between mountains and the ocean. In December 1999, following a huge rainstorm, floods surged down the slopes and through the towns, sweeping victims into the ocean.

DEBRIS FLOWS

The rain caused deadly landslides that buried several villages. It also caused debris flows—a dangerous mixture of water, mud, boulders, tree branches, and wreckage from buildings that were already destroyed. The debris makes the flood especially deadly.

◄ Torrential rains in 2005 caused more flood damage in Vargas state.

FLASH FLOODS

The Vargas disaster was a flash flood—a sudden, fast-moving flood that's often unexpected. Flash floods happen most often when heavy rain collects on steep slopes, or fills up mountain streams.

MOZAMBIQUE FLOODS

In 2000, a huge flood hit Mozambique. It was caused by weeks of heavy rain, not in Mozambique, but in neighboring South Africa and Botswana. The rain drained into the mighty Limpopo and Zambezi Rivers, which flow through Mozambique.

◀ This survivor escaped the floods by climbing onto a chimney.

DESTRUCTION RATING

Devastating for most of Mozambique's farming areas.

BORN IN A TREE

One woman, Cecilia Mabuiango, was heavily pregnant when she climbed up a tree during the floods. After waiting there for three days with no food or drinking water, her baby was born! Eventually, they were both rescued by a helicopter, and survived.

WATERWORLD

The floods covered a huge area of low-lying farmland, destroying crops and killing thousands of cows, as well as hundreds of people. Because there were few high buildings in the area, people escaped up trees or onto bridges, and later had to be rescued by boat or helicopter.

▶ Flood survivors are airlifted to safety.

NORTH SEA FLOOD

In 1953, a windstorm in the North Sea, combined with an unusually high tide, created a disastrous storm surge that flooded parts of the United Kingdom, Germany, Belgium, and the Netherlands. It happened on the night of January 31, and the water was ice cold.

◄ Dutch workers team up to repair a dike, built to keep seawater out of the Netherlands.

▲ Houses in the Netherlands were swamped by deep water during the deadly 1953 flood.

NEW DEFENSES

The deadly sea flood led these countries to build much better flood defenses, and the disaster has not been repeated. But, as sea levels are now rising, seawalls may have to be raised.

NO WARNING

Although the Dutch weather service did forecast the storm, most radio stations in 1953 didn't broadcast at night, and few people heard the warning. They woke up to find freezing water filling up their homes, sometimes as high as the second story. Along the coast of Scotland and England, 307 people were drowned or died from the cold. Then the storm crossed the English Channel and caused devastating floods in the Netherlands and Belgium, where 1,863 people died.

RED RIVER DELTA

Vietnam's Red River has a system of dikes and barriers—some of them 1,000 years old—to prevent flooding. But the monsoon rains of summer can easily overfill the river. On August 1, 1971, there was so much rain that the defenses failed, causing a catastrophic flood.

DESTRUCTION RATING

Although little is known about it, this was one of the world's worst floods.

MYSTERY FLOOD

We know this was one of the most serious floods in history, with about 100,000 people killed, huge areas of rice crops destroyed, and a major city, Hanoi, severely swamped. But not much else is known about it—mainly because in 1971, Vietnam was in the middle of the violent Vietnam War between North and South Vietnam (now one country). Not much news could get out, and there are hardly any photographs of the flood.

▲ The water of the Red River is colored by the earth that washes into it.

ST. LUCIA'S FLOOD

In 1287, a storm surge in the North Sea caused a flood that changed the shape of a country, the Netherlands. At high tide, the seawater broke through a dike or seawall, and so much water rushed in that it created a whole new area of the North Sea.

DESTRUCTION RATING

This vast flood was one of the most destructive ever.

▲ The huge, modern IJsselmeer dam now protects the Netherlands from the seawater.

AMSTERDAM GROWS

The flood deluged towns and villages, and 50,000 people died. It was called St. Lucia's flood because it happened on December 14, the day after the holiday known as St. Lucia's Day. The new sea, called the Zuiderzee, or South Sea, reached right up to the village of Amsterdam, allowing ships to sail there easily. The village became a port, and it gradually grew into a large city, now the capital of the Netherlands.

BELOW SEA LEVEL

Today, a new, much bigger dike has been built to keep the sea out. What was the Zuiderzee has become the IJsselmeer, a freshwater lake below sea level. About 20 percent of the country's land is also below sea level. This means it is at risk of flooding, but the modern dikes are much bigger and stronger than the old ones.

GROTE MANDRENKE

The name of this catastrophic 1362 flood, Grote Mandrenke, is Dutch for "great drowning of men." It began as a huge storm that tore across northern Europe, blowing down trees and church spires in Ireland and England, before crossing the North Sea. On January 16, it caused a huge storm surge.

NEW ISLANDS

In the Netherlands, the high water rushed inland, making the Zuiderzee, created by the 1287 storm surge, even bigger. It also washed away large areas of land, creating lots of new islands along the coast. Existing islands were reshaped, and some ended up half the size they had once been. The floods also killed about 25,000 people.

▼ The power of the North Sea has always been a danger in the Netherlands.

DESTRUCTION RATING

Another catastrophic flood disaster for the Netherlands.

▼▲ Pottery finds have given us clues about life in Rungholt.

GOOD-BYE, RUNGHOLT

Rungholt, an important trading port in the north of the Netherlands, was completely washed away, along with its population of about 2,000. For centuries afterward, artifacts and ruins of the town were found in the North Sea—and, according to folklore, when you sail over it, you can still hear the church bells ringing.

NORTH INDIA FLOODS

In June 2013, Uttarakhand state in northern India was soaked by a sudden, super-heavy downpour. As the rivers filled up and overflowed, their banks collapsed. Riverside houses, hotels, and roads fell in and were washed away, bridges broke apart, and whole villages were flattened.

DESTRUCTION RATING

A short but deadly flood disaster.

STRANDED PILGRIMS

As it was summertime, pilgrims and tourists had flocked to the remote, mountainous area to visit its holy shrines and temples. So many roads and bridges were lost that up to 100,000 people became stranded. They had to wait several days with hardly any food until they could be rescued by helicopter. Thousands more people sadly died.

▲ A survivor is helped along the remains of a mountain road washed away by floodwater.

NATURAL DISASTER OR MISTAKE?

After the disaster, some environmental experts said it could have been avoided. To meet the needs of the tourist industry, roads, bridges, and hotels had been built quickly, many of them too close to rivers or in frequently flooded areas.

CHICAGO SEICHE

Just what is a seiche? It's a bit like a storm surge, but in a lake or enclosed harbor, rather than an ocean. It happens when something pushes the water one way, and it starts to slosh backward and forward.

SEICHE ON LAKE MICHIGAN

▶ The major city of Chicago stands on the shore of stormy Lake Michigan.

The Great Lakes of America and Canada are at risk of seiches, and one of the worst happened on Lake Michigan in 1954. It struck at 9:30 a.m. on June 26, and there was no warning. As the seiche passed the city of Chicago, the water level suddenly rose by 10 feet (3 meters). Eight people who were fishing on a pier were instantly washed away and did not survive. Because it was during the hot summer, many more people would have been there if the seiche had hit later in the day.

▼ Lake Michigan, 1954

DESTRUCTION RATING

Seiches can kill, but don't usually cause a major disaster.

WHAT CAUSES A SEICHE?

Seiches are actually very common, but they only get noticed if they are unusually large. Wind can cause a seiche, and so can a landslide. Earthquakes can cause them, too, especially in swimming pools.

Wind ⟶   Storm water level

INDIAN OCEAN TSUNAMI

HOW TSUNAMIS WORK

A tsunami happens when a landslide, volcanic eruption, or earthquake suddenly moves a large amount of water. The biggest tsunamis are usually caused by earthquakes that happen under the ocean.

Water is sucked back **Tsunami**

Underwater earthquake

On December 26, 2004, at about 8:00 a.m., a giant magnitude-9, mega-thrust earthquake shook the seabed close to Indonesia. The earthquake itself was bad enough, but the tsunami it caused was the worst in history. It spread around the Indian Ocean, and killed more than 200,000 people.

INDIA | **Banda Aceh**
Indian Ocean
INDONESIA

BEFORE

▲ ▶ Part of the city of Banda Aceh, Indonesia, before and after the tsunami.

AFTER

INDIAN OCEAN

The tsunami reached Indonesia first, where huge waves, up to 80 feet (24 meters) high, swept away whole towns. As the waves traveled farther from the epicenter, they eventually caused disaster in Thailand, India, and Sri Lanka, and even reached the east coast of Africa. The Pacific Ocean, where tsunamis are quite common, had a warning system in place, but the Indian Ocean did not, so most people had no idea the tsunami was coming.

DESTRUCTION RATING

The deadliest tsunami ever, causing terrible destruction all around the Indian Ocean.

GREAT TOHOKU TSUNAMI

When the people of Tohoku in northeastern Japan felt a powerful earthquake on March 11, 2011, they knew what to do. Fearful that a tsunami would follow, people began running to higher ground. An hour later, it arrived.

▼ Ocean water pours over a sea wall, washing away cars and signposts.

TERRIBLE TSUNAMI

This huge and frightening tsunami shocked the world, especially as many people on roofs and hilltops managed to video it arriving. First, the ocean was sucked back, leaving beaches empty—a sign that a tsunami is about to strike. Then, it roared back, and waves up to 130 feet (40 meters) high poured over seawalls and tore through the streets, carrying cars, trees, and wrecked buildings with them. In some places the water flowed 6 miles (10 kilometers) inland. About 18,000 people did not survive.

TSUNAMI ALERT!

Tsunamis washed ashore around the rest of the Pacific Ocean, too. But they were much smaller than those that hit Japan, and this time a tsunami warning system was in place.

▼ The tsunami waves washed this big ship ashore.

DESTRUCTION RATING

Destroyed a large, heavily populated area of Japan, and damaged a nuclear power station.

LITUYA BAY MEGA-TSUNAMI

Few people saw the tallest tsunami on record, which is probably good, considering experts think it was 1,720 feet (524 meters) tall! It happened in 1958 on the coast of Alaska, when an earthquake caused a huge landslide to crash into the ocean at the top of Lituya Bay, creating the monster wave.

RIDING THE WAVE

Howard Ulrich and his 7-year-old son were on their boat in the bay. They described how a huge wave moved down the bay, lifting their boat up and carrying it over the trees, before they ended up floating on the ocean again.

DESTRUCTION RATING

Destructive to trees, but did not affect many people or built-up areas.

▶ The pale areas on the lower parts of the banks are where the wave stripped away trees from the 9-mile (14.5-kilometer) long bay.

TRAIL OF TREES

Although the tsunami couldn't be measured at the time, scientists have determined its size from the scars it left on the shore. The water swept away all the trees from the banks of the bay as it went by, leaving them bare. An extraordinarily large tsunami such as this is known as a mega-tsunami. However, it was also a local tsunami, meaning it only affected a small, local area.

▼ The wave was five times taller than the Statue of Liberty in New York City.

Statue of Liberty

ALEXANDRIA TSUNAMI

In 365 CE, a massive earthquake struck under the Mediterranean Sea near the island of Crete. The quake sent a deadly tsunami racing south toward Egypt, where it swamped the ancient city of Alexandria, killing 50,000 people.

▶ Alexandria's famous lighthouse survived the tsunami.

EYEWITNESS: AMMIANUS

A Roman historian, Ammianus, described the tsunami, including the way the sea retreated before the wave arrived: "The sea was driven away, its waves were rolled back, and it disappeared ... many-shaped varieties of sea-creatures were seen stuck in the slime ... People wandered at will ... to collect fish and the like in their hands; then the roaring sea rises back in turn ... For the mass of waters returning when least expected killed many thousands by drowning."

DESTRUCTION RATING

One of the ancient world's most famous and disastrous tsunamis.

BENEATH THE WAVES

This earthquake and tsunami were part of a series of events that slowly ruined ancient Alexandria. Today, the modern city is on Egypt's coast, while the ruins of the old city lie under the sea.

▶ Divers search for artifacts from the sunken city of Alexandria.

ENSHUNADA TSUNAMI

In 1498, a powerful sea earthquake just off Japan's coast sent a tsunami up to 56 feet (17 meters) high surging inland in the Nankaido area. It ruined several towns and killed about 30,000 people. It also permanently changed the coastline.

◄ The statue of the Buddha is still there today, and is popular with tourists.

THE GREAT BUDDHA

The tsunami hit the town of Kamakura, home to a famous giant statue of the Buddha (founder of the Buddhist religion). The 42-foot (13-meter) tall statue used to sit inside a large temple building, but the tsunami washed the temple away—even though it was 0.6 miles (1 kilometer) inland. The statue also survived the Great Kanto Earthquake of 1923 (see page 25).

▼ You can see a model of a catfish in this Japanese festival float.

WRIGGLING CATFISH

According to Japanese folklore, earthquakes and tsunamis are caused by a giant catfish called Namazu, who lives in the mud under the islands of Japan. A god named Kashima is said to hold the catfish still with a stone, but once in a while he breaks free and wriggles, causing an earthquake.

EUROPEAN TSUNAMI

Tsunamis hardly ever happen in Europe—but one did, in November 1755, after the huge Lisbon earthquake (see page 27). Some coasts were swamped by 66-foot (20-meter) high waves. Even in Cornwall, in southern England, the waves were up to 13 feet (4 meters) high.

Lisbon earthquake epicenter

ROUND TWO?

Experts think another earthquake off the coast of Portugal will happen one day, so North Africa and northern Europe could face another tsunami. Some experts believe these areas should have a tsunami warning system like the Pacific Ocean does, just in case.

DESTRUCTION RATING

Destruction severe to Portugal, decreasing as it moved farther away.

LA PALMA TSUNAMI

Some experts fear that La Palma, one of the Canary Islands in the Atlantic Ocean, could cause a tsunami if its volcano erupts and triggers a major landslide. This tsunami could be very large, affecting Europe, Africa, and the United States.

▲ As well as crossing the Atlantic, the waves curved away from Portugal and back toward Africa and Europe.

▼ In Galway, Ireland, the tsunami destroyed half of the town's Spanish Arch. Only two of the original four spans are still standing.

Spanish Arch

LAKE TAHOE TSUNAMI

Lake Tahoe is a big lake in the Sierra Nevada mountains between California and Nevada. It's a beautiful spot and a popular tourist attraction, not somewhere you'd expect to meet a tsunami. But scientists think that thousands of years ago, there was a tsunami at Lake Tahoe.

▶ The lake is calm now, but imagine a giant tsunami roaring across it!

DESTRUCTION RATING

This tsunami must have been horrendously destructive to any creatures living there.

LAKESIDE LANDSLIDE

Studies of the lake show that, sometime within the past 20,000 years, a huge chunk of rock slipped away from the side of the lake at McKinney Bay, and plunged to the bottom. This caused a huge tsunami, probably about 330 feet (100 meters) high. As it was in an enclosed lake, it would have become a huge seiche, surging back and forth over the shores.

QUAKE WARNING

The landslide was probably caused by an earthquake, and seismologists say that another quake could happen in the area, causing another tsunami. Although it may not be very likely, scientists are studying the lake and the land around it, so they can predict what might happen.

ARICA TSUNAMI

▼ Arica is famous for its steep hill called Morro de Arica.

The Arica tsunami was one of many originating from earthquakes along the west coast of South America. In 1868, the town of Arica, now in Chile, was part of Peru. On August 13, at about 5:00 p.m., a ginormous quake shook the seabed just off the coast.

ARICA'S MORRO

The earthquake destroyed the town. But worse was to come. It also shook the huge, steep hill, called the Morro, that stands over Arica, causing a landslide that buried the ruined town. You can still see the Morro (with its changed shape) today.

▼ One of the ships, the USS Wateree, after it was carried ashore.

THREE SHIPS

Several ships were in Arica's port. The crews saw the earthquake happening. Then they felt the ocean begin to move. It drew back, then surged up high and poured ashore in a tsunami estimated to be 90 feet (27 meters) high. Three large ships were hurled far inland, and what was left of Arica after the earthquake and landslide was swept away by the water.

DESTRUCTION RATING

A terrible earthquake and tsunami that together killed at least 25,000 people.

LAKE MONOUN

On August 15, 1984, people living near Lake Monoun in Cameroon, Africa, heard a loud rumbling coming from the lake. People walking in the area found themselves in a strange cloud of gas. Many fell unconscious, and dozens suffocated and died.

▼ The area beside the lake where the deadly gas collected.

▲ Villagers gather on the lake after the disaster.

LAKE MONOUN MYSTERY

At first, no one knew what had caused the disaster, and some thought it might be a deliberate attack. In fact, the gas was carbon dioxide, and it had come from Lake ... The lake is in a volcanic area, and

HIGH AND LOW

Carbon dioxide gas is heavier than air, so when it is released, it flows downhill. It collects on the ground and pushes the normal, oxygen-rich air out of the way. This meant the effects were worst for people in low valleys nearby, who suddenly found they could not breathe. A truck driving through the gas broke down, because engines need oxygen to work. However, people riding high up on top of the truck were unharmed.

LAKE NYOS

A much bigger limnic eruption than Lake Monoun's happened at Lake Nyos, Cameroon, on August 21, 1986. The lake began to bubble loudly as gas suddenly burst out of it. This created a tsunami wave more than 65 feet (20 meters) high.

GAS PIPES

To try to prevent another deadly limnic eruption in Lake Nyos, scientists have installed degassing pipes. These allow the carbon dioxide to bubble up safely and slowly from the bottom of the lake.

▼ A scientist at Lake Nyos collects samples from a degassing pipe.

▼ After the limnic eruption, the waters of Lake Nyos appeared brown and muddy.

GAS FLOOD

This eruption released a huge amount of carbon dioxide, mixed with other volcanic gases. These flowed down and covered a large area of land, reaching as far as 16 miles (25 kilometers) away. Many villages were affected, and the gas killed 1,700 people, as well as thousands of cows.

DESTRUCTION RATING

A very rare and serious disaster.

71

VAIONT DAM DISASTER

Terrifying disaster still used as a warning to student engineers.

The Vaiont (or Vajont) dam in Italy, completed in 1960, was built to provide hydroelectric power. As it was being built, experts warned that Monte Toc, a mountain close to the dam, might collapse. Did anyone listen? No.

▼ Water poured down the valley without warning or time to evacuate.

▶ At 860 feet (262 meters) high, the Vaiont dam was the tallest in the world in 1960.

THE BIG ONE

In late 1963, after several small landslides, a much bigger one began to move down Monte Toc. The dam's owners decided to empty out some of the water, but they did not get rid of enough. On October 9, the whole side of the mountain suddenly plunged into the reservoir behind the dam. This created a mega-tsunami 820 feet (250 meters) high that roared over the top of the dam. The villages in the valley below were swamped, and 2,000 people died.

WHAT CAUSES LANDSLIDES?

A landslide is a large amount of soil or rock slipping downhill. Landslides are most common on steep slopes, especially those made of sandy or loose rock. If rain soaks such a slope, it makes the soil and rock much heavier, which can result in a landslide. Earthquakes or volcanic eruptions that shake the ground also set them off.

YUNGAY LANDSLIDE

A horrifying natural disaster happened in 1970. On May 31, a large earthquake in the seabed off Peru's coast shook and badly damaged the Ancash area. But even worse, the quake loosened a huge chunk of rock and glacier on Peru's highest mountain, Huascaran.

▼ Huascaran's debris landslide filled the valley below.

DESTRUCTION RATING

A huge and devastating landslide.

ICE SLIDE

A huge wave of rock, dust, ice, and mud (made as the ice melted) tumbled down the mountain and spread out across a valley. The flow was almost 0.6 mile (1 kilometer) wide, and moved at a mind-boggling 200 miles (350 kilometers) per hour—as fast as a high-speed train. In just a few minutes, it reached the town of Yungay and the nearby village of Ranrahirca. Both were engulfed and destroyed. Almost all of Yungay's 25,000 people died. Only a few hundred survived by running uphill to the town's cemetery, which the landslide did not quite reach.

MEMORIAL TOWN

The town of Yungay was rebuilt nearby, but the remains of the old Yungay, including a crushed bus and the ruins of the cathedral, were left as a memorial park.

▼ Part of old Yungay's church still stands as a reminder of the disaster.

DISASTER RECORD
Peru's worst-ever natural disaster.

MONT GRANIER LANDSLIDE

If you visit Mont Granier in the French Alps today, you'll see that it has a huge, sheer cliff face on one side, as if half of the mountain just fell off. Well, it did!

▼ Mont Granier, France

BASE JUMPING

There are several mountains with sheer cliffs around the world, including the Eiger in Switzerland and El Capitan in California. These mountains are popular with BASE jumpers, who like to parachute off high places, such as buildings, cliffs, and high bridges, as a sport.

▲ A BASE jumper makes a dangerous daredevil leap.

CLIFF COLLAPSE

This monster medieval landslide happened on the night of November 24, 1248. No one knew much about what caused landslides then, but today scientists think it happened because of the weight of limestone rock resting on weaker, slippery "marl" rocks. As the mountain fell down, it crumbled into a river of rock and mud that flowed over five whole villages and parts of two more. It's thought that several thousand people were killed.

STOREGGA SLIDE

The Storegga Slide was the biggest landslide ever known. Where did it happen? Under the North Sea off the coast of Norway, at least 7,000 years ago. It was so huge that it shifted 840 cubic miles (3,500 cubic kilometers) of rock and mud.

THE TSUNAMI

The landslide was a thousand times bigger than the biggest-ever landslide on land (the collapse of Mount St. Helens in 1980, see page 11). Because it was underwater, this landslide didn't fall on top of anyone. However, it was still very deadly, because it caused a tsunami that rippled around the North Sea and caused devastation along the shores of Scotland and England. We don't know how many people were affected, but scientists have found evidence that the water rolled up to 50 miles (80 kilometers) inland in parts of Scotland.

ISLAND BRITAIN

The Storegga Slide may have been what finally separated the United Kingdom from the rest of Europe by washing away the last remnants of "Doggerland." This was a large area of marshland that once connected the United Kingdom to what is now France, Belgium, Germany, and the Netherlands.

NORWAY

Doggerland

UK

FRANCE

ARMERO LAHAR

A lahar is a fast-flowing river of mud. Lahars usually form when a volcanic eruption combines with water, and the sticky mud flows down the mountain. One of the worst-ever lahar tragedies occurred in Armero, Colombia, in 1985.

▲ A rescue helicopter plucks a survivor from the Armero mud.

▶ The deadly, fast-flowing mud swamped the whole town.

SLEEPING VOLCANO

The disaster was caused by the eruption of the Nevado del Ruiz volcano on November 13, 1985, after it had been dormant for many years. Although experts had warned of the dangers, people were not evacuated. Armero itself was 45 miles (70 kilometers) from the peak. But the eruption melted snow on the volcano, creating huge lahars that poured down the valleys. More than two hours later, the mud rushed over Armero, killing thousands.

HIGHER GROUND
If people had known the mud was coming, they could have simply escaped to the hillsides. Today, many countries have advanced lahar warning systems to prevent another disaster such as Armero from happening again.

DISASTER RECORD
The deadliest lahar in history.

TANGIWAI LAHAR

On December 24, 1953, a wall of ice and rock holding up one side of the crater lake at the top of Mount Ruapehu in New Zealand suddenly gave way. Water, sand, and silt mixed together to form a muddy lahar that poured downhill into the Whangaehu River.

▲ The crater lake of Mount Ruapehu.

LAHAR WATCH

Mount Ruapehu still poses a lahar risk today, but it now has a warning system. In 2007, another similar lahar occurred, but everyone was evacuated and the railroads and roads were closed.

DESTRUCTION RATING

Though not a huge lahar, it had deadly consequences.

BRIDGE CALAMITY

An express train from Wellington to Auckland was heading toward the Tangiwai railroad bridge across the river. Just minutes before it arrived, the lahar struck the bridge and washed away one of its pillars. A passing motorist spotted the damage and used a flashlight to warn the train driver. The driver braked, but the front part of the train went onto the bridge, which collapsed, and five train cars fell into the river. The guard and motorist managed to rescue almost everyone from the sixth train car before it, too, fell in. The lahar claimed 151 lives.

▲ A train crosses the Tangiwai bridge after the 2007 lahar.

WINTER OF TERROR

An avalanche is like a landslide, but made of snow. Avalanches are common in steep, snowy mountain ranges, especially the Alps. When a huge amount of snow slips down a mountain at high speed, it can bury walkers, skiers, houses, and whole villages. One of the worst winters for avalanches on record was 1950–51.

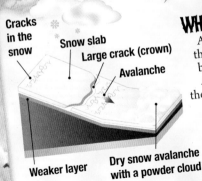

Cracks in the snow

Snow slab

Large crack (crown)

Avalanche

Weaker layer

Dry snow avalanche with a powder cloud

▲ This diagram shows how an avalanche happens.

WHAT CAUSES AN AVALANCHE?

An avalanche can happen wherever there is so much snow piled up that it becomes too heavy to support itself. Avalanches can also be triggered by the movement of skiers or snowmobiles, an earthquake, a glacier shifting, or by wind.

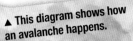

DESTRUCTION RATING

A disastrous wave of avalanches.

TERRIBLE WINTER

Avalanches claim a few lives every year, but during the 1950–51 "Winter of Terror," almost 270 people lost their lives in the Swiss and Austrian Alps. There were 649 avalanches, which destroyed hundreds of buildings, flattened forests, and killed huge numbers of animals.

◄ Rescuers arrive to dig out snow-covered houses in the winter of 1950–51.

WHITE FRIDAY

White Friday is the name given to a disastrous day during the First World War, when hundreds, possibly thousands, of soldiers died in the Italian Alps—not from fighting, but because of avalanches.

DESTRUCTION RATING

This shocking disaster may have been the worst avalanche ever.

▶ Troops in 1916 haul guns across the snowy mountains.

10,000 DEAD?

Many reports claim that 10,000 soldiers died on White Friday, but there are no detailed records, and we don't know for sure. Some estimates say it's more likely to be between 1,000 and 2,000—which would still make this one of the deadliest avalanche disasters ever.

FRIDAY THE 13TH

The day now known as White Friday was Friday, December 13, 1916, when troops from several countries were stationed in Italy's mountains. On this day, a vast area of unstable snow on Mount Marmolada collapsed, causing an avalanche that flattened an Austrian army camp, killing at least 300 men. Many other deadly avalanches happened the same day, and during the rest of December, and the war made it especially difficult to organize rescues.

IRAN BLIZZARD

You might expect the world's worst-ever blizzard to have happened somewhere such as Alaska. In fact, it took place in Iran, a country that is often very hot. It began on February 3, 1972, and went on for seven days.

AS HIGH AS A HOUSE

As more snow fell, it covered towns and villages up to a depth of 26 feet (8 meters). People sheltering in their homes ended up trapped inside, while others outdoors were buried by snow. Trains were halted, telephone lines snapped, and roads were blocked. Rescuers tried to reach people by helicopter, but about 4,000 did not survive.

▼ The Iranian city of Isfahan, covered with snow.

▼ Snow on the mountains of Iran.

WHAT IS A BLIZZARD?

A blizzard can happen when there is lots of heavy snowfall and strong winds at the same time. The wind blows the snow around so that it fills the air in a "whiteout," and snow piles up in deep drifts. Unable to see where they are going, people can get stuck and die from the cold—even though they may not be far from safety.

DESTRUCTION RATING

Devastated a huge area and destroyed 200 villages.

DISASTER RECORD
The worst blizzard on record.

AFGHANISTAN BLIZZARD

Afghanistan in Central Asia is used to snow—heavy snow falls every winter, and when it melts in spring and summer, it provides a water supply for the country. But the snows of February 2008 were far worse than normal, and became a deadly blizzard.

▶ An Afghan man takes a walk in the snow.

FROSTBITE

As temperatures fell to -8°F (-22°C), people began walking through the snow and ice to try to reach safety, often in bare feet. This led to many cases of frostbite, which happens when toes, fingers, hands, feet, or the tips of noses get too cold, freeze, and turn black.

SNOW

Snow more than 6 feet (2 meters) deep covered large parts of the mainly mountainous country, including mountain villages and farms, where many people were living in basic, one-story houses and huts. The blizzard cut off roads to these villages, leaving people without food and the fuel they needed to keep warm. More than 900 people died, as well as hundreds of thousands of sheep, goats, and cows.

▲ Badly frostbitten body parts can turn black, and in some cases have to be removed.

1998 ICE STORM

Most storms are noisy, but an ice storm can be eerily quiet. They happen when cold rain freezes onto cold objects. In the ice storm that struck Canada and the northeastern United States in 1998, the ice was up to 4 inches (10 centimeters) thick.

▲ Heavy ice snapped this power tower in 1998.

▼ This tree branch, weighed down with ice, fell onto and crushed a car.

DEADLY STORMS

Ice storms can cause traffic accidents, leave people trapped and freezing cold for many hours, and sometimes leave dangerous live power cables lying on the ground.

DESTRUCTION RATING

Caused widespread destruction and more than 30 fatalities.

ICE STORM DANGERS

The 1998 ice storm went on for five days, starting January 5 and ending January 9. The ice collected on all sorts of surfaces—roads, road signs, roofs, trees, and power lines. The weight of the ice made this very dangerous. Tree branches broke, and roads became blocked or were too slippery to use. Many people were stuck in their homes with no electricity, heating, or drinking water—because all the pipes had frozen—and many farm animals starved, or died when their barns fell down under the weight of the ice.

IDAHO ICE STORM

This famous ice storm hit Idaho from January 1 to 3, 1961. Freezing rain and thick, freezing fog filled the area and helped the ice to build up to record levels.

▼ The ice was so thick and heavy that it brought down wires.

GLAZE AND RIME

When water freezes fast, it creates milky-white, crusty ice called rime. When it freezes more slowly, it forms a thick, clear coating, known as glaze.

▼ ► Rime on trees (right) and glaze-covered twigs (below).

STUCK IN THE ICE

Vehicles, houses, trees, roads, and power lines were all covered in so much ice that the whole area was brought to a standstill. Almost everyone affected by the storm lost their power supply for days, and many cars, homes, and other buildings were badly damaged. It was after this ice storm that electricity companies began developing new, stronger systems for supporting power lines to try to prevent future serious blackouts.

SYDNEY HAILSTORM

If a hailstone the size of a pea hits you, it can hurt. So imagine what it was like for the people of Sydney, Australia, in 1999, when hailstones 3.5 inches (9 centimeters) across started falling on them!

▶ The damage to property made this the most expensive natural disaster in Australia's history.

HOW HAIL HAPPENS

Hailstones form when ice builds up around specks of dust caught in stormclouds. Updrafts—winds that blow upward inside the clouds—stop the balls of ice from falling until they get so big and heavy that they can't be held up anymore. The more powerful the storm, the bigger the hailstones can be.

▲ The storm front gathers over Sydney in 1999.

HAILSTONE HOLES

Some people even claimed they saw hailstones up to 5 inches (13 centimeters) across! The hailstones came zooming down—some at 120 miles (200 kilometers) per hour—and smashed holes in 20,000 roofs, 40,000 vehicles, and at least 25 planes at Sydney airport. Although people were injured in car crashes and cut by breaking glass, nobody was badly hurt.

▲ This diagram shows hailstones forming inside a stormcloud.

MUNICH HAILSTORM

One of Europe's worst-ever hailstorms hit Munich, Germany, on July 12, 1984. The storm featured strong winds, heavy rain, and hailstones the size of tennis balls!

HAILSTONE DESTRUCTION

The storm injured about 400 people. Some were cut as car windshields got smashed, some were hit by shattered glass from windows, and others were injured by the hailstones themselves. About 70,000 homes were damaged, along with more than 150 aircraft and 200,000 cars. For years afterward, cars with big dents in them were a familiar sight in the city. The damage cost Germany more than any other natural disaster.

◄ After the storm, the sidewalks were ankle deep in broken roof tiles.

▼ A deep layer of huge hailstones collected on the ground.

SURVIVE A HAILSTORM

Hailstorms with giant hailstones are rare, but here's what you should do if you ever get caught in one:
- If possible, get indoors and stay there!
- If you're in a car, stop and park safely. Lean away from the windows and cover yourself with a blanket or a coat.
- If you're stuck outdoors, curl up in a ball and cover your head and neck with your arms. Getting under a tree may provide some shelter.

DESTRUCTION RATING

One of the most powerful hailstorms on record.

ST. LOUIS HAILSTORM

The St. Louis hailstorm of April 10, 2001, was a monster storm. It formed just west of Kansas City, Missouri, then tracked eastward for eight hours, traveling 360 miles (580 kilometers) to St. Louis and the neighboring town of Florissant.

Missouri

▲ This map shows the 2001 hailstorm's long, narrow path, or "hail swath," through Missouri.

▼ Sometimes lots of small hailstones clump together and form a giant lump, as in the huge Vivian hailstone below.

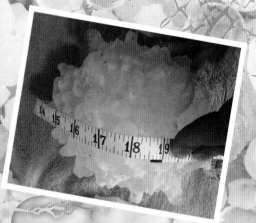

BIGGEST HAILSTONE EVER

The largest hailstone on record fell at Vivian, South Dakota, in 2010. It was about 8 inches (20 centimeters) across, and weighed just under 2 pounds (1 kilogram).

SMASHED CARS

The storm moved across two cities and a heavily populated area, hurling hailstones as it went—some as big as baseballs! On its way, the hailstorm dented more than 60,000 cars, including hundreds of brand-new ones outside car factories. Aircraft and houses also got damaged. In some places, winds blowing straight downward made the hail smash to the ground even faster.

ROOPKUND HAILSTORM

High in the Indian Himalayas lies Lake Roopkund. In 1942, at least 300 human skeletons were found in its icy water and around its edge. In summer, when the ice melts, preserved bodies can even be seen in the water— so what happened here?

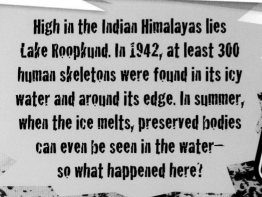

▲ The strange, shallow lake has many broken skeletons scattered around it.

THE KING'S TRIP

Legend says that long ago, the king of Kannauj, 190 miles (300 kilometers) to the south, came here on a religious pilgrimage with a large retinue of servants, but all of them died when they were caught in a sudden storm of giant hailstones. For decades few people believed this, and it was thought the bones may have belonged to soldiers from World War II. But in 2004, scientists found that most of the people at the lake had died from hard, heavy, round objects falling onto their heads. A hailstorm really was to blame!

OLD BONES

The scientists dated the skeletons and their belongings, such as shoes and jewelry, to about 850 CE. This means they had been lying by or in the lake for 1,200 years. Since their rediscovery, tourists have begun taking the bones away.

PESHTIGO

Wildfires usually happen in hot, dry weather in parched forests or grasslands. The Peshtigo fire of 1871, in and around Peshtigo, Wisconsin, was one of the worst wildfires ever.

▶ The firestorm burned with intense heat and raced toward Peshtigo, shown here in 1871, before the fire.

▼ An old illustration of the deadly Peshtigo fire, showing people trying to escape.

DRY SUMMER

After a hot, dry summer, the people of Peshtigo were hoping for rain. On Sunday, October 8, strong winds began to pick up. Small fires, lit to clear land or burn litter, were blown out of control and set the dried-out forests on fire. The fire became a firestorm—a huge, high, roaring wall of fire. It engulfed a wide area, including the town of Peshtigo. It also caused fire tornadoes—spiraling towers of fire and wind that can drag cars and trees into the air. About 2,000 people died.

INTO THE RIVER

Many people ran into the cold waters of the Peshtigo River to escape the flames, but this was deadly, too. Some drowned trying to stay underwater to avoid the heat and smoke. Others stayed in the water so long that they got too cold and died of hypothermia.

INDONESIA FOREST FIRES

In 1997, in Indonesia, fires that were started deliberately to clear farmland got out of control. Fanned by dry, windy weather, they were impossible to put out, and became the biggest wildfire disaster in history.

HAZE HORROR

In Indonesia itself, the fires burned vast areas of farmland and forests that were home to rare and protected wildlife, as well as people. But that wasn't all. The smoke from the fire caused a dangerous haze or smog that spread right across southeast Asia, affecting other countries such as Malaysia and Thailand. The smog caused air and road accidents, ruined crops, and made people ill. No one knows how many died as a result, but it may have been thousands.

▶ People had to wear face masks to protect themselves from the thick smog.

▼ A plane dumps water on Indonesia's peat fires to try to put them out.

PEAT FIRES

The fires also spread to peat bogs, where peat is dug out of the ground to use as a fuel. Peat fires burn slowly, and are very hard to put out. Many are still burning in Indonesia today.

BLACK SATURDAY

Black Saturday was a tragic wildfire disaster in Victoria, Australia, on February 7, 2009. After a heat wave with temperatures up to 116°F (47°C), the forests were hot and dry, and strong winds were coming. The state banned all fires to try to prevent a disaster—but this failed, and dozens of fires broke out.

▼ A raging wildfire seen from the air.

▲ A badly burned forest after the 2009 bushfire.

WILDFIRE CAUSES

When conditions are very hot and dry, the following things can start a dangerous fire:
- Wind blowing power lines down, creating electric sparks
- Sparks made by machinery or power tools
- Dropped cigarette stubs
- Lightning
- Curved broken glass concentrating the sun's heat like a magnifying glass
- Campfires or picnic fires that spread or aren't properly put out
- Fires started deliberately to cause damage

OUT OF CONTROL

All afternoon, deadly wildfires (called bushfires in Australia) and firestorms raged across the state. They destroyed or damaged thousands of houses, leaving at least 7,000 people homeless. Almost 200 people died, and hundreds more were hurt. Thousands of firefighters worked for weeks to put out the fires, but they only managed this once the weather cooled and rain fell.

GREECE WILDFIRES

The summer of 2007 was the hottest and driest that Greece had ever experienced—creating perfect conditions for wildfires to start. In a period of less than three months, the country had 3,000 fires.

GREECE

Smoke from fires

▶ A satellite image shows smoke from the 2007 fires in Greece.

▼ This wildfire was photographed from the Athens suburb of Parnitha.

GREECE ON FIRE

The wildfires burned all over the country, destroying parks, farmland, and houses. They burned the forests and suburbs around Athens, Greece's capital, and threatened the site of Olympia, where the Olympic Games were held in ancient times. Fortunately, most of Olympia survived. Firefighters fought hard to control the flames with specially designed planes and helicopters that dump water onto the fires from above. However, 84 people died, and thousands lost their homes.

DESTRUCTION RATING

A disastrous summer for Greece.

BRESCIA 1769

It's rare for people to get struck by lightning, and even more rare for lightning to cause a major disaster. But this is exactly what happened in Brescia, Italy, in 1769.

◀ The explosion would have been seen for miles.

▼ Bell ringers in the past were at risk from lightning running down the bell ropes.

DESTRUCTION RATING

A terrible disaster caused by one lightning strike.

SAFE AS A CHURCH

Churches were used to store explosives because they were large, strong buildings, and also because the ringing of church bells was (incorrectly!) believed to ward off lightning. Many bell ringers died while ringing church bells during thunderstorms to keep the lightning away.

GUNPOWDER CHURCH

At the time, churches didn't have lightning conductors to carry the electrical charge safely to the ground. So when lightning struck the church of St. Nazaire, it set the church on fire. Unfortunately, the church's vaults had 200,000 pounds (90,000 kilograms) of gunpowder stored in them. The gunpowder blew up in an enormous explosion, a sixth of the city was destroyed, and some 3,000 people were killed.

FLIGHT 508

A plane being struck by lightning isn't usually dangerous, but for LANSA Flight 508 it was. The plane was flying over Peru on December 24, 1971, when it entered a thunderstorm. Suddenly, lightning struck one of its wings and set fire to a fuel tank, and the plane fell apart.

▼ Flight 508 was a Lockheed L-188A Electra turboprop similar to this one.

ARE PLANES SAFE?

Today, all planes are designed with lightning in mind. They are built so that the electrical energy will flow around the outside of the aircraft and escape safely. Lightning strikes on aircraft are actually quite common, but do not tend to cause problems.

ONE SURVIVOR

The plane crashed into the Peruvian rain forest. Amazingly, one person, 17-year-old Juliane Koepcke, found she had survived the fall—she was still in her airplane seat. She managed to make a ten-day trek along a river in the forest, surviving on candy, before she found some local people who rescued her.

▼ Juliane Koepcke in 1972

93

2003 HEAT WAVE

Can a hot summer really be a natural disaster? A period of unusually high temperatures, called a heat wave, might sound like a good thing if you like summer weather, but it can be incredibly dangerous—as deadly as some of the biggest natural disasters of recent times.

DESTRUCTION RATING

A major weather disaster.

▼ Red on this map shows unusually hot areas in 2003.

UK

FRANCE

SPAIN

EFFECTS OF HEAT

Heat waves can be dangerous because they cause the following problems:
• Heatstroke—this makes you get so hot that you stop sweating and get confused and dizzy. It can be deadly.
• Dehydration—not drinking enough liquid can lead to exhaustion and collapse.
• Air pollution—this can make people with breathing problems very ill.

EUROPE IN THE HEAT

In August 2003, a record-breaking heat wave settled on Europe, especially France. Temperatures reached above 100°F (40°C) for days on end. In the United Kingdom, it was the first time a temperature this high had ever been recorded. While some people enjoyed the heat, it led to a huge increase in deaths, especially among the elderly and sick. In fact, it's now thought that the death toll was more than 50,000. But, because the effects of a heat wave happen gradually and are widespread, they often cannot be measured until much later.

2010 HEAT WAVE

Another serious heat wave happened in the summer of 2010, this time centered on Eastern Europe and Russia. It's thought this heat wave was even more deadly than the one in 2003, and was Russia's hottest summer for over 1,000 years.

MORE HEAT WAVES?

Scientists think that global warming will make heat waves more common in the future. A heat wave such as the one in 2003 could eventually happen every couple of years.

SUN, SMOG, AND FIRE

At least 15,000 people in Moscow alone died from the heat, smog, and poor air quality. The heat wave also caused droughts, water shortages, and dangerous forest fires. In Germany, passengers aboard a full train had to be rescued, and many of them taken to hospital, after the air-conditioning broke down and temperatures inside the train soared. Meanwhile, in the Arctic Ocean it was so hot that a giant chunk of an ice shelf broke off and floated away.

◀ During a heat wave, people often swim in unusual places, such as this fountain in Moscow.

▼ In Moscow, smog and smoke from wildfires made the air difficult to breathe.

DESTRUCTION RATING

One of the worst heat waves ever.

NORTHERN CHINESE FAMINE

In 1875, a four-year drought began in northern China. Lack of rainfall meant crops didn't grow well, and there were severe water shortages for people and animals. Millions of people died as a result.

▼ A starving family receives aid in 1910.

▼ China had another serious drought in 2013.

DISASTER RELIEF

This was one of the first natural disasters to have an international relief effort, organized by British and Chinese religious groups, charities, and businesses. They reported on what was happening and set up appeals for donations of money and help, which saved millions of lives.

MULTIPLE WHAMMY

The drought caused a famine—a disastrous food shortage—that lasted from 1876 to 1879. Running out of food and water, people began to die of starvation. Some resorted to eating grass, tree bark, and soil, which often made them ill. Being thin and undernourished, many caught deadly diseases, such as typhus. People also died fighting over food supplies. It's thought that the death toll from this famine was at least 13 million people.

DOJI BARA FAMINE

Every summer, India depends on heavy monsoon rains for its water supply. But from 1789 to 1792, the monsoon rains never came. This caused a terrible drought, leading to the famous Doji Bara famine of 1791 to 1792.

FAMINE

People were reduced to eating leaves and roots, and selling all their possessions. Some were so desperate they ate rotting animals that lay in the fields. Local leaders tried to import extra food and deliver it to the famine zone, and people donated food to the poor, but this wasn't enough to prevent about 10 million deaths.

EL NIÑO

The reason the monsoon rains didn't come was probably because of an El Niño event. El Niño is a warming of water in the Pacific Ocean off the coast of South America. It happens every two to seven years, and has an impact on weather around the world, causing storms, floods, and droughts in different areas.

▶ A woman carries water home across a dried-up lake bed in 2003.

MAYAN MEGA-DROUGHT

A drought may last for just one or two weeks, or for several years. But some droughts go on for decades, or even hundreds of years. These "mega-droughts" can be seen as a kind of climate change that affects human history. Some experts think the great Maya civilization of Central America declined because of a mega-drought.

▶ One of the famous pyramids built by the Maya.

BY THE SEA

Some parts of the Maya civilization did survive longer, especially in northern coastal areas. This could be because people were able to survive on seafood. Droughts usually affect large, inland areas more than coastal regions.

After — decline

Before / decline   CENTRAL AMERICA

◀ The map shows the homeland of the Maya.

THE MAYA

The Maya people dominated Central America from ancient times until about 1000 CE. They had calendars and writing systems, and were great builders—their records show the dates of their monuments and buildings. From about 800 CE, however, the Maya began to build less, and their major cities declined. Climate studies suggest this could have been because of a mega-drought that lasted for several hundred years, ruining their water supply and farming. Cutting down trees to make space for their cities and farms probably made things worse, allowing the dry soil to blow away.

DESTRUCTION RATING

No one can be sure how bad or deadly the drought was, but it may have helped to destroy a civilization.

DUST BOWL

The Dust Bowl was a famous, decade-long drought and disaster that hit the United States in the 1930s. It was partly a natural disaster, caused by high temperatures, strong winds, and lack of rain, but it was also partly caused by poor farming.

▲ The map shows the area, in red, known as the Dust Bowl.

▼ The Black Sunday storm looked like a monstrous black cloud moving along the ground.

DUST DISASTER

The central prairies were once used to graze cattle, but in the 1800s and 1900s the land was plowed and crops were planted. This meant there was no grass to hold the soil down. So when a huge drought hit, from 1931 to 1939, the soil just turned to dust, and the wind blew it away in giant dust storms. Facing terrible food and water shortages, more than three million people trekked west to look for work. Thousands suffered from deadly "dust pneumonia," which damaged their lungs, and others died from the intense heat.

BLACK SUNDAY

Black Sunday was the name given to April 14, 1935, when one of the worst dust storms of all blew through the Dust Bowl. Eyewitnesses described how it was too dark to see, cars had to stop, small animals suffocated, and birds thought it was nighttime and flew to the trees to roost.

WINTER PARK SINKHOLE

Imagine a hole in the ground suddenly opening up under your feet. In Florida, this happens fairly often! The holes, called sinkholes, happen when underground rock, usually limestone, gets worn away by water. If a big hole develops just under the surface, the ground on top can fall in.

DESTRUCTION RATING

This sinkhole made a big impact because it happened in a town, but luckily no lives were lost.

▼ This sinkhole grew to be about 330 feet (100 meters) wide and 90 feet (27 meters) deep.

◄ A large section of road, an auto body shop, and several vehicles all fell in.

SWALLOWED UP

One of Florida's most famous examples was the Winter Park sinkhole of 1981. On May 8, Mae Rose Williams heard a strange swishing sound in her yard. It was the sound of a hole opening up in the ground. After a few hours, the hole had grown much bigger and swallowed up a tree. The next day, Rose evacuated her house just before it, too, fell in.

LAKE ROSE

At first, tourists flocked to see the hole and it became a national news item. Later, the bottom was lined with concrete, and it filled up with water to form a lake— now named Lake Rose after Mae Rose Williams.

BEREZNIKI SINKHOLE

Berezniki in Russia is plagued by sinkholes— a problem partly caused by humans. The city is built on top of a system of mines, and when underground water flows through them, it dissolves some of the rock that the city rests on, making the surface collapse.

▲ A crack from a sinkhole outside the Berezniki mine construction office.

SINKHOLE SPOTTING

The government of Berezniki has set up a system of 24-hour video cameras to try to spot sinkholes as they start, so that anyone in danger can be evacuated. But some people think it's time to move the whole city and rebuild it somewhere else.

DESTRUCTION RATING

The town has not been destroyed so far, but it is in danger.

▲ The gaping Grandfather sinkhole in Berezniki. Yikes!

THE GRANDFATHER

The biggest sinkhole in Berezniki, nicknamed "The Grandfather," opened up in 2007, and kept on growing. It is more than 1,300 feet (400 meters) long, 980 feet (300 meters) wide, and 780 feet (230 meters) deep—that's deep enough to hold a 70-story building! The hole is in danger of swallowing up a railroad and a warehouse.

GUATEMALA SINKHOLES

▼ In 2011 this deep hole opened up under someone's bed!

This terrifyingly scary-looking sinkhole is in Guatemala City, in Central America. It opened up suddenly on May 30, 2010, swallowing up a three-story factory. And it wasn't the city's first hole!

DANGER ZONE

Guatemala's sinkholes claimed several lives, but there could have been many more casualties if a busy workplace, school, or shop had been affected. Scientists are working to try to predict or prevent any more sinkholes.

DESTRUCTION RATING

These deadly sinkholes also destroyed property and streets.

▼ The huge 2010 sinkhole is about 66 feet (20 meters) across and 100 feet (30 meters) deep.

ALTO

UNA VIA

WHAT HAPPENED?

A similar, even deeper sinkhole appeared in 2007—and experts think there could be more in the future. The deep holes appeared after a flow of underground water dissolved the ground under the city. Instead of hard limestone, the city is built on loose, grainy pumice rocks and ash from old volcanic eruptions. These wash away easily, sinking into deeper underground cracks. Water from broken water pipes and heavy rains eroded the rocks.

DOOR TO HELL

This amazing sinkhole in Derweze, Turkmenistan, isn't just big and deep—it's on fire! It's been burning for more than 40 years, and is nicknamed "the Door to Hell!"

DESTRUCTION RATING

Luckily, no one has been harmed because the hole appeared in an empty area of desert.

▼ The burning pit of fire is horribly hot inside.

HOW BIG?

The giant, dish-shaped hole is about 230 feet (70 meters) across and 70 feet (20 meters) deep.

▲ Tourists trek to this remote area to see the mind-boggling sight.

NONSTOP GAS

The sinkhole used to be an underground cavern filled with natural gas. Scientists discovered it in 1971 while looking for underground oil reserves. But when they drilled into the ground to try to extract the gas, the roof of the cavern caved in, and large amounts of methane gas began to leak out. To stop the gas from polluting local villages, it was set on fire in the belief it would soon burn off and go out—but it hasn't!

103

1859 SOLAR STORM

On September 1, 1859, astronomer Richard Carrington was studying sunspots—temporary dark areas on the sun's surface—when suddenly a solar flare shot out from the Sun. Seventeen hours later, Earth was hit by a powerful solar storm.

GOING WRONG

The solar storm had a powerful effect on electrical equipment, which was quite a new invention. There were no electronic computers, phones, or TVs, but there was an early form of electric communication—the telegraph. It relied on a signal being switched on and off, but this stopped working because the telegraph wires were so highly charged with extra electricity.

AMAZING AURORAS

That night, people were amazed to see incredibly bright displays of aurora borealis (Northern Lights) and aurora australis (Southern Lights), caused by the surge of particles hitting Earth's atmosphere. Instead of being visible only near the poles, as usual, they could be seen all over the world, almost to the equator.

▶ Auroras can be almost as bright as day.

▼ A solar flare is a huge mass of energy and charged particles that shoots out from the sun.

◀ In the 1800s, telegraph operators such as these sent messages across long distances.

2003 SOLAR STORM

Solar flares are actually very common, but most of the time they shoot off away from Earth. It's rare for a really big solar flare to point right at us. In recent times, the biggest one to affect Earth happened on November 4, 2003.

DESTRUCTION RATING

Not as bad as it could have been.

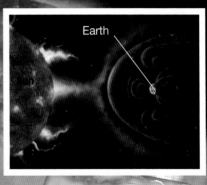

Earth

▶ This diagram shows how a solar flare slams into Earth's magnetic field.

THE BIG ONE?

The problems caused by the 2003 solar flare weren't too bad, but some scientists think a really big solar flare in the future could be disastrous. It could cause huge power cuts, interfere with air traffic control signals, and mess up the electronic systems we use to control money and communications.

▲ The 2003 solar flare, captured on camera by a space telescope.

STORM DAMAGE

Modern astronomy equipment can predict solar flares and storms before they arrive, so in 2003 scientists knew the surge of energy might damage technology on Earth, as it had in 1859. Sensitive pieces of electronic equipment on space satellites and in telescopes were turned off to keep them safe. There was a power cut in Sweden, radio transmissions and GPS signals were disrupted, and some aircraft had to be redirected, but there were no great disasters.

TUNGUSKA EVENT

On June 30, 1908, people in central Russia saw a strange, fiery object moving across the sky. A huge explosion followed, near the Podkamennaya Tunguska River. The bang was so enormous that its shock wave blew people into the air and broke windows 50 miles (80 kilometers) away. What had happened?

▶ Part of the asteroid and the trees flattened by the impact.

▲ This artist's impression shows the asteroid hurtling toward Russia.

EXPLODING ASTEROID

It was almost 20 years before scientists visited the site. There, they found that a vast area of forest—about 80 million trees—had been flattened. All the fallen trees were pointing outward, away from the middle of the area. The scientists determined that an asteroid or comet from space had fallen to Earth, but exploded before landing, probably about 4 miles (6 kilometers) up. This disaster is now known as the Tunguska Event.

ASTEROID DANGER

The impact on the trees showed that if this explosion had happened over a city or a very populated area, it could have killed millions. Today, astronomers look out for asteroids so that if any are heading toward Earth, we might have time to evacuate the danger zone.

YUCATAN ASTEROID

▲ The Yucatan peninsula is circled in red.

A massive ancient crater lies half in and half out of the ocean on Mexico's Yucatan peninsula. The crater measures 110 miles (180 kilometers) across. It was discovered in the 1960s and 1970s by scientists studying rocks. They realized it must have been made by something huge crashing into Earth.

▲ An artist's impression of the asteroid splashing down.

DESTRUCTION RATING

Possibly destroyed the dinosaurs and changed the history of our planet.

◄ *Triceratops*, one of the last dinosaur species, was wiped out by this event.

HOW BIG?

To make a crater this big, the object—probably an asteroid, but possibly a comet—must have been at least 6 miles (10 kilometers) across! Some scientists think it was even bigger.

PREHISTORIC DISASTER

Scientists interested in what caused the dinosaurs to die out about 66 million years ago—an event known as the K/T extinction—thought a big asteroid impact must have been the cause. Debris would have darkened the sky for years, leading to a food shortage that could have wiped out large animals. Eventually, studies showed that the Yucatan asteroid struck at exactly that time. Now, most scientists agree that the asteroid was to blame for the K/T extinction.

GLOSSARY

ancestors People who lived a long time before us.

asteroid Rocky object that orbits the sun.

avalanche Mass of snow and ice slipping downhill.

caldera Big, wide crater left by an exploding volcano.

comet Space object made of ice and dust.

cyclone Spiraling storm, such as a hurricane, that forms in the Indian Ocean.

debris flow Fast-flowing mixture of water, rock, mud, and rubble.

dike An embankment or long wall built to hold back water.

drought Long period of low or no rainfall.

earthquake lights Flashing or colored lights sometimes seen before an earthquake.

earthquake swarm Series of earthquakes and tremors.

epicenter The point on Earth's surface directly above an earthquake.

eruption Release of lava, ash, or gas from a volcano.

extinction Dying out and no longer existing.

famine Long, serious food shortage that causes starvation.

fault The area where two of the tectonic plates in Earth's crust meet.

firestorm Fast-burning wildfire that sucks in air currents, which make the fire burn more fiercely.

fire tornado Tall, whirling column of wildfire.

flash flood Sudden, local flood.

frostbite Damage caused when body parts freeze.

geyser Natural fountain of hot water from underground.

glacier Huge river of ice that flows slowly downhill.

hail swath Path of a hailstorm across the land.

hurricane Spiraling storm found in the Atlantic Ocean.

hydroelectric dam Dam that uses the flow of water to generate electricity.

lahar Fast-flowing river of mud.

lava Molten rock that flows out of a volcano.

levee Barrier built to hold back a large body of water.

limnic eruption Sudden escape of gas from a lake.

liquefaction When shaking makes the ground behave like a liquid.

magma Molten rock found inside Earth.

monsoon Seasonal wind in Asia that brings heavy rains.

pyroclastic flow Fast-flowing river of rocks, ash, and gas from an erupting volcano.

seiche "Sloshing" effect in a lake or pool.

sinkhole Hole that opens up suddenly in the ground.

smog Smoky air pollution.

solar flare Burst of energy out of the sun's surface.

solar storm The effects on Earth made by a solar flare.

stratovolcano A type of volcano with thick lava and explosive eruptions.

sunspots Dark spots that form on the sun's surface.

tectonic plates Huge sections that make up Earth's crust.

tornado Narrow, extremely fast whirling windstorm.

tremor Slight shaking of the ground felt before or after an earthquake.

tropical storm Another name for a cyclonic storm.

tsunami A powerful wave caused by a sudden disturbance of water.

typhoon Spiraling storm found in the Pacific or Indian Oceans.

vent An opening in a volcano.

volcanologist Scientist who studies volcanoes.

waterspout Whirling column of water caused by a windstorm, such as a tornado, over water.

wildfire Out-of-control, damaging fire in a forest, scrubland, or wilderness.

INDEX

ACKNOWLEDGMENTS

The publisher thanks the following agencies for their kind permission to use their images.

Key: t=top, b=bottom, l=left, r=right

Cover Images:
Shutterstock © Igor Zh (front, main), Valderzrl (front, top), Solarseven (back, main), Ammit Jack (back, inset top)

Alamy
21 © Mark Pearson, 21bl © Robert Harding Picture Library Ltd, 26 © age fotostock Spain, S.L., 27 © North Wind Picture Archives, 29 © ClassicStock, 41 © Niday Picture Library, 45b © US Marines Photo, 47 © RGB Ventures / SuperStock, 47cl © Stocktrek Images, Inc., 53bl © Top Photo Corporation, 58 © Frans Lemmens, 65cl © Falkensteinfoto, 72cr © Marka, 73cr © Maxime Dube, 74 © Christophe Diesel Michot, 74cr © Photos 12, 78 (background) © Galen Rowell/Mountain Light, 81 © Mark Pearson, 81br © Images & Stories, 82 © Megapress, 85 © Interfoto, 85cl © Interfoto, 90 © bildbroker.de, 101 © ITAR-TASS Photo Agency, 107cr © Science Photo Library

Corbis
4–5 © Corbis, 7tl © Corbis, 11 © Corbis, 12 © FULLY HANDOKO/epa, 13 © CORBIS, 23 © Jim Sugar, 23br © Mark Downey, 24cl © Imaginechina, 25 © Bettmann, 25cl © Hulton-Deutsch Collection, 31 © Bettmann, 33 © TWPhoto, 34b © (C) Guo Jian She / Redlink/Redlink, 37 © SIMON BAKER/Reuters, 39 © Bernard Bisson/Sygma, 42 © Frederic Soltan/Sygma, 44 © Wu Shuibin/Xinhua Press, 44tr © Imaginechina, 45 © Herman R. Lumanog/NurPhoto/NurPhoto, 47br © David Muench, 49bl © Stringer/Reuters, 52cr © Julia Waterlow/Eye Ubiquitous, 53 © STRINGER SHANGHAI/Reuters, 55 © Reuters, 55br © Reuters, 56cl © Bettmann, 60 © Stringer/India/Reuters, 63 © AFLO/Nippon News, 63br © Per-Anders Pettersson, 65br © Reuters Photographer / Reuters, 70 © Louise Gubb, 70cr © Louise Gubb, 71 © Thierry Orban/Sygma, 71cr © Louise Gubb, 72 © Bettmann, 73 © Lloyd Cluff, 76c © Jacques Langevin/Sygma, 77 © Anthony Phelps/X01468/Reuters, 82tr © Christopher J. Morris, 84cr © Corbis, 87 © Ocean, 88cr © Bettmann, 89 © Michael S. Yamashita, 89b © Michael S. Yamashita, 90cl © Country Fire Authority/Xinhua Press, 93br © Bettmann, 94 © Reuters, 96tr © Board of Foreign Missions/National Geographic Society, 97r © Reuters, 102 © STR/Reuters, 102tr © JORGE DAN LOPEZ/Reuters, 104 © Paul Hardy

Getty Images
10 Steve West, 12 br LightRocket via Getty Images, 20 Stocktrek, 20cr Gamma-Rapho via Getty Images, 30 Getty Images, 32 Sovfoto, 34cl ChinaFotoPress, 36 MCT via Getty Images, 36cl Christian Kober, 46tr Getty Images, 50cl Christine Pemberton, Gallo Images, 54 © STR/Stringer, 56 The LIFE Picture Collection, 57 Bruno De Hogues, Photographer's Choice, 61cr Getty Images, 65r De Agostini, 67b Design Pics / The Irish Image Collection, Perspectives, 76 Gamma-Rapho via Getty Images, 78bl Getty Images, 79 UIG via Getty Images, 80 Kelly Cheng Travel Photography, Moment, 84 Fairfax Media via Getty Images, 88cl (map) Historic Map Works, 91tr Getty Images, 91 Getty Images, 92cr Getty Images, 106cr UIG via Getty Images

NASA
17tr (r) NASA/GSFC/METI/ERSDAC/JAROS, and U.S./Japan ASTER Science Team, 38bl Jeff Schmaltz, MODIS Rapid Response Team, NASA/GSFC, 42cl NASA and the Joint Typhoon Warning Center, 44bl NASA/MODIS Rapid Response, 91cr NASA Earth Observatory, 94cr Image courtesy Reto Stockli and Robert Simmon, based upon data provided by the MODIS Land Science Team, 104br NASA/SDO/AIA, NASA/STEREO, SOHO (ESA & NASA), 105 NASA/ESA, 106cl Leonid Kulik Expedition, NASA, 107 NASA/Don Davis

NOAA
50 Dr. Joseph Golden, NOAA, 64 NOAA's Historic Coast & Geodetic Survey, 67tr NGDC Global Historical Tsunami Database, 83cr NOAA's National Weather Service (NWS) Collection, 86bl NOAA, 99 NOAA Photo Library, Historic NWS collection, 100bl NOAA/NGDC, A.S. Navory,

Photoshot
18 © Andia, 20bl © Photoshot/TIPS, 48br © Xinhua, 52 © Xinhua, 96 © Xinhua, 100 © Photoshot, 101tr © Photoshot

Science Photo Library
17tr (l) David Hardy, 22cr Claus Lunau, 37cl Gary Hincks, 62cl Digital Globe, Eurimage, 62cr Digital Globe, Eurimage, 77tl Dr Richard Roscoe, Visuals Unlimited, 84bl Gary Hincks, 106 Joe Tucciarone

Shutterstock.com
1t achapo, 1b solarseven, 2bl Eugene Sergeev, 2-3 Ammit Jack, 6bl Nigel Spiers, 7tl Rainer Albiez, 7cr solarseven, 8br Byelikova Oksana, 13tr T photography, 14 Graeme Knox, 14tl AridOcean, 14br TyBy, 15cl JCElv, 15 Tokelau, 16 Carlos Amarillo, 16br ivan bastien, 17 (sky) Olympus, 17 bl leoks, 17cr Ralf Siemieniec, 18bl TyBy, 19 Lorcel, 19cl AridOcean, 24 AridOcean, 28 alexkatkov, 28cl Morphart Creation, 31tr Photoraidz, 32bl Mikael Damkier, 35 Yai, 35bl Maciej Bledowski, 40 (background) toadberry, 40cb Volina, 41cl Fotoluminate LLC, 43 AridOcean, 46 (background) Minerva Studio, 46cr AridOcean, 48 (sky/tornado) solarseven, 48 AridOcean, 49 (sky) S.Borisov, 49 Matt Jeppson, 51 solarseven, 59 Oskari Porkka, 59 cl Dario Lo Presti, 59 bl Sibrikov Valery, 61 Oleksandr Koretskyi, 61b PILart, 62 (background) Christian Weber, 62tl Designua, 64bc chuckstock, 64bl Matthew Cole, 66 Curioso, 66br Aduldej, 67 (background) Nejron Photo, 68 topseller, 69tr Inga Locmele, 69 (background) Nejron Photo, 75br Anton Balazh, 78cl Designua, 80cr Prill, 82 (background) Leonid Ikan, 86 (background glass) Uka, 86 (background hail) Andrzej Sliwinski, 86tr bahareh khalili naftchali, 87br (long bone) sNike, 87br (skull) revers, 88b art-pho, 90t (flames) VanderWolf Images, 90cr Ziablik, 92 LukaTDB, 92cl Simon_g, 93 Johnny Lye, 95 Sergey Gordeev, 95cc Don Mammoser, 97b Designua, 98 Christian Delbert, 98cl Filip Bjorkman, 98cr Peter Hermes Furian, 99cl AridOcean, 103bl Lockenes, 104bl Marzolino, 105cr Aaron Rutten, 107tr Filip Bjorkman

Superstock
38 Coast Guard Public, 75 Water Rights/Water Rights

Others
8 Parker & Coward, Britain; 9 Jialiang Gao (peace-on-earth.org), 9cr Uwe Dedering (Wiki), 12tr Dan Dzurisin (U.S. Geological Survey), 22 Arnold Genthe, 34tr Mistman123 (Wiki), 40 Elliott, William, Lt (artist & publisher); Green, Valentine (engraver), 54tl David Rodrigues, 69b Courtesy of Murray Greene Day, U.S. Naval Historical Center Photograph, 83 Richardfabi (Wiki), 83bl Nicolas M. Perrault, 93cl San Diego Air and Space Museum Archive (Wiki), 103 Tormod Sandtorv